LOVE IN AND OUT OF LOCKDOWN

40+ ideas & activities for a healthy relationship
during a global pandemic

EDEN E. WOLFE   CHRISTINE NISAN
ANAÏS DANESI

Chiens & Chat Press

Disclaimer

This book is designed to provide information and motivation to readers. It was developed with the understanding that the authors are not engaged to render psychological, legal, or any other kind of professional advice. This book is not intended as a substitute for counseling. The content of each chapter is the sole expression and opinion of its author.

No warranties or guarantees are expressed or implied by the authors' and publishers' choice to include any of the content in this volume. Neither the publisher nor the individual authors shall be liable for any physical, psychological, emotional, financial, or commercial damages, including, but not limited to, special, incidental, consequential or other damages.

No part of this book may be reproduced in any form or by any electronic or mechanical means, including information storage and retrieval systems, without written permission from the author, except for the use of brief quotations in a book review.

Some names and identifying details have been changed to protect the privacy of individuals.

Contents

Part V

HOW FUN CAN WE MAKE THIS?
ROCKING THE LOCKDOWN AND LIFE THEREAFTER

PART I

ARE YOU KIDDING ME? THE ARRIVAL OF LOCKDOWN

Pandemic-Proofing our Relationships

The man on the TV announces that the lockdown is coming. We don't know how long it'll last, but it's going to be a while. At least six weeks. I'm guessing at least eight. But nobody really knows.

I look over to my husband who is playing his balalaika (a Russian instrument that looks a bit like a giant nacho chip with strings) and I can't help thinking, what's this going to do to us as a couple? (Spoiler Alert: We survive! More on that throughout the book...)

Fast forward four months. FOUR MONTHS. The heavy lockdown where we live lifted almost completely... And we're still married! Not only that, but we're stronger than we were before... Okay, we went through some challenges, and we had it easy compared to some other couples we know (we both already worked from home and we don't have children). But we used the opportunity to reflect and talk with our friends in similar situations.

What did we do? How did we get through it still loving each other? What was it that made the bad times so hard? And what are we going to do differently next time?

We all know it could happen again at any time. My husband and I figure this is not the last time we'll be confined together.

Relationships are hard. And yet, we're also hardwired for them. I remember a good friend, older, who had been married for many decades and when she talked about tough times in her marriage, I asked, "So how long did those last? Bad weeks? Bad months?"

"There were bad years," she said.

That was a wakeup call for me.

There were days during lockdown when I woke up and immediately thought, "There's no way I'm getting through this day without exploding on someone or something."

And then there were days when at 8pm I stepped on the balcony to applaud the healthcare workers - which my neighborhood did every night for three months - and I thought, "I am so lucky, blessed, and privileged to be alive."

And then there were days when I was sure death was coming for us.

Maybe you've experienced some similar thoughts and feelings on the rollercoaster of this wild period in our history. Maybe you're still experiencing them. And maybe you experience them with a partner living in close quarters. If so, this book is for you.

Or maybe you're in a new relationship, that budding love that's fresh with fun and discovery, and you think you might be living together when the next lockdown happens. If so, this book is for you.

Maybe your relationship is rock solid. Maybe you love learning about your partner and want to play around with some new approaches to living in close quarters during a global pandemic. Yep, this book's for you.

This is a book of tips and tricks. Ideas and concepts. Games and activities. Working on relationships can be hard. It is particularly hard during health pandemics and lockdowns. With this book, we provide you with some ways to make the time, journey and situation as meaningful and fun as possible, too.

These Are Not Normal Times

We can't start this book without reiterating what must be painfully obvious for us all. **Nothing is as it was.** And furthermore, we can pretty much be sure that nothing will quite be the same again. The world in which our relationships were created is not the one we're now living in.

What does that mean for us? It means that our abilities to adapt, be flexible, and accept change are more important than ever. But many of us have had to become experts at these skills in a short timeframe.

There are some great resources on personal adaptation, and our recommended list has some of them. That is a whole science that goes far beyond the pages of this book. So, let's simply say this: we're all going to need to learn to adapt and transform at a rate that many of us have never before experienced, and change is HARD. It's hard. It's painful. And for our relationships to survive, change is absolutely necessary.

Our relationships may have thrived on physical activity, travel, or even simply spending more time apart than together.

But the world has changed.

Perhaps it used to be that when your partner annoyed you, you went for a walk, went shopping, played a game of ball with the dog, or visited your friends.

But the world has changed.

We all will have to admit, first to ourselves and then possibly to others as well, that we do not have all the answers.

It also means that the traditional ways of doing things do not bring the same outcomes that they used to.

We have to reinvent our relationships in this new reality and rediscover our reasons for being together, because perhaps even those very reasons may have changed.

This new normal will usher in periods of vast uncertainty – not the least in terms of financial, professional, and mental as well as physical health. So this is the time to find out what really are the roots of our relationship and to grow new branches that will take us forward from here.

Indeed, these are not normal times, but we can't be sure than normal as we knew it will ever exist again. In the meantime, we continue to live with our partners, husbands, wives, families, and we've got to find a way to live well together - not just to survive but to grow and thrive.

That's where this book may come in handy.

————

Activity

Make a list of each aspect of your life which has changed because of the pandemic. Once it is written, tuck it away somewhere so that you can revisit it at a later time and check in with yourself as time goes by.

————

Questions for Reflection

What has changed for me personally during this pandemic?

What has changed for us as a couple?

Are any of these welcome changes? What do I miss most?

Making the Best Use of this Book

Each chapter offers a unique piece of insight, a concept, an idea, an activity and reflection questions. Questions for reflection can be done individually or in a couple. They can be shared with friends. And most importantly, *they don't have to be answered.*

The act of considering them is enough.

But if you *can* answer them, you might be able to find some actionable items that are the best fit for your life.

Several chapters have suggested activities. These activities vary in their approach. Some require conversation, others are simply fun.

Some will challenge you to do things differently, now that we live in a world that is different from the one we knew.

These activities are not magic.

Some will not be right for you, or for your partner, or for you both as a couple. Even though they aren't guaranteed, some just might shine some light into places that have been dark during lockdown and in the days since new government policies allowed you to move about outside.

We hope these activities will help continue building your relationship the way it has for those of us who have given them a try already.

What This Book Doesn't Cover

Since we couldn't do everything with this book, we wanted to be clear about some of its limitations:

- This book is not a 'how-to' for an always awesome, amazing relationship during a global pandemic. We wish we had all the answers to keeping relationships at 100% all the time. We don't.

- This book will not work for everyone. There will be ideas in here that resonate with you - give them a shot. There will be things in here which you think "no freaking way!" That's okay, too. This book is intended to prompt reflection and creativity. If something isn't for you, just let it go.

- This book is focused on couples *without* young children. That is a whole other kit and caboodle, which we believe requires its own book!

- This book is not 'professional help'. During these trying times, there are relationships that need professionals who are trained to deal with significant and complex relationship issues. We provide some advice on how to find these people at the end of the book.

- This book is not a peer-reviewed journal article with cutting edge scientific methods for reviving your relationship. We are just everyday, regular folk with our own individual experiences and stories, and with professional experiences that are relevant to this book. We also include stories from those who were willing to share. Some research, a bunch of personal experience, and a solid investment in listening have formed the basis of our recommendations.

- This book is not the definitive relationship book. But it will offer tools, stories, and resources that apply specifically to relationships in this strange time.

Keeping It Real: Some not-so-great ways to relate

Right off the bat, we thought it would be useful to provide an at a glance summary of some bad ideas for relating - in general, whether in a pandemic or not.

No matter how tempting it is, don't:

1. Go through your mental rolodex of all injustices or snubs you believe that your partner has inflicted and point them out on a regular basis.

2. Be sarcastic. Usually, sarcasm is an insult disguised as wit. It can be painful, frustrating, erode trust, and over time, build contempt.

3. Comment negatively about your partner's weight gain or loss. We all deal with change and stress in different ways. Some naturally lose weight. Some find solace in a 'no carbs left behind' diet. The bottom line is that your partner might not be *feeling* their best, so let it go.

4. Disparage your partner's appearance. We are talking here about personal grooming and overall appearance. Perhaps you

like to lounge in jogging pants and your comfy bathrobe. Perhaps they like to dress up, even while at home. Perhaps you prefer to grow out your beard and she prefers to let the hair grow everywhere. The important thing is to let each other be. Ask yourself, does it *really* matter?

5. Attach yourself to your partner like Velcro. Everyone needs their space, especially when they are close quarters for months on end. Wanting to know what your partner is doing at all times, insisting on being right beside them, and following them around is not conducive to finding balance. If you would like to be able to offer affection because you're overflowing with cuddles and snuggles during this time, consider fostering a dog who would love that constant connection.

6. Provide a play-by-play of alarming and distressing news about the pandemic (unless this is something that you and your partner enjoy doing together). Some people like to know what's happening and to follow the news and daily updates. Others do not. The key is to respect your partner's wishes. If they prefer not to know, do not insist on telling them.

7. Complain. Complain and then complain some more. Purging complaints on your partner – about the lockdown, the weather, the political situation, all the various stressors of your work and life – may be difficult for them and increase their anxiety. They might absorb the negative energy and feel deflated while you may feel better for airing it out. We are not suggesting that you not talk about things that bother you. By all means, do so in a constructive manner, with an eye towards improvement. However, complaining as a pastime can wear thin rather quickly. If this is how you process things, try writing in a journal (see the chapter on journaling) or venting to friends and family who don't mind being an ear.

8. Give the silent treatment. It's quite possible that while you think you are punishing your partner through silence, they might actually see it as a welcome gift. However, it is not a good strategy, neither in or out of lockdown. It can breed frustration, anger, hostility and make you both feel lonely. If you are not ready to talk, try writing notes or letters. Tell your partner you are not yet ready to talk, but once you've processed the issue, then the two of you can have a discussion. Simply going on silent mode without any warning or staying that way will only create distance, and that distance may increasingly become harder and harder to bridge.

9. Withhold affection and sex. We've all done it. It is only natural that you don't want the very person you are pissed off at to touch you. However, once you begin to use withholding sex as a weapon, it can easily become a tool of control and power play, leading to feelings of rejection, frustration and anger. *We have the right not to be touched, even by our partner.* It is quite possible that the stress of the pandemic and lockdown have lowered your libido and you are simply not in the mood. This is perfectly fine and understandable. Bring your partner into the discussion and share these feelings. Now, if it is a matter of 'you get no affection because I am punishing you,' see if there are other more productive ways to address your feelings and resolve your issues.

10. Let your partner do all or most of the chores without pitching in. There are still things to do around the house. There are groceries to pick up, cooking to do, and dishes to wash. There is still laundry, vacuuming, watering plants, managing the finances, and cleaning bathrooms. Is this work shared? Do you find that you 'let' your partner do the lion's share of the housework? Perhaps this is an arrangement you've made and it works out fine – then, no problem. However, if

you're both working from home or if your partner resents having to do all the housework, then why not help out? As a wise man once told my husband – washing the floors is a potent aphrodisiac.

11. Shove this book under your partner's nose and say, "You do this and this and this." If your partner does indeed do some of these things, approach it kindly and constructively. And be kind to yourself if you see yourself reflected in some of the messages we share.

6

A Lockdown Love Story: Surprise! I'm moving in!

Jolan and I met when I was nearing the end of a sixteen-month trip in an RV (Recreational Vehicle, or camper van for some) across North America. I was nearing the end of my trip, I had sold my RV, and I was in Montreal, Canada, at a hostel that had a hot tub on the roof.

Jolan arrived on the same day as me and was in bed opposite from me in a dorm of 10, though there was only one other person there.

One day we hit it off and spent some great time together, with some surprising chemistry. We are not really romantic people, kind of the opposite of that, but a deep and unexpected connection grew between us in those few weeks.

Although we kept in touch, I didn't really expect us to become a thing. After all, he lived in Belgium and I was moving back to the south of France.

But after a couple of months back in Europe, we met up. And then we met up again. And next thing we were an official couple. We moved between countries every few weeks but we were still in the early days, having fun and seeing what would come.

I learned the lockdown was coming just a few days before it was going to happen. Jolan didn't think there would be a lockdown at all. But when it did, we figured it would last a few weeks, but we didn't like the idea of not being able to see each other.

I called Jolan and asked, "Should I come to Belgium?"

Let's just say, he wasn't totally into the idea. Though he wasn't against it either.

Would I be invading his space? What if it didn't work out? What if we were stuck together?

I spent the entire night tossing and turning, asking myself if it was a good idea. Should I stay or I should go?

The president of France was going to come on TV on Monday, announcing the lockdown. So I finally decided on Sunday that I would go to Belgium and we'd figure the rest out. If really it went bad, I figured that I could still come back to my own country. Driving 700 miles by car seemed like the best option, as it would allow me an escape back home in my car if it was needed. (I must note that on European standards, 700 miles is *very* far!)

I called him and explained my idea, and he said, "Uh, okay."

Clearly, he still wasn't sure.

I was changing all of my work arrangements, canceling patients and trying to figure out the work side, while also quickly throwing stuff randomly into my suitcase.

I filled the gas tank, knowing if wouldn't be enough for the eleven-hour journey.

And would they stop me at the border?

Since the president was going to speak on Monday night, I figured I just had to get there before the borders closed.

Jolan was pretty sure none of it was going to happen - no lockdown, no closing borders - but, well, he was wrong!

There were so many little details to consider, like where was a safe place for my car, how to handle costs, and such. I kept going over the various details in my head as I drove.

On the way I called him *three times*, just to make sure he still wanted me to come. He said yes, but I wasn't convinced.

On my last call, he said, "You're on your way now, so just come."

I was nervous. But I hoped for the best.

And the good news was there was no one on the roads! I still got there pretty late at night and was exhausted.

After about ten days we managed to find our rhythm. He continued to work even during lockdown. I took two weeks off because at that time I didn't have the right to see patients over video conference.

We'd never considered living together, and suddenly we had to learn all the basics about each other. What do you like to eat? When? What time do you go to bed? All that stuff that young couples go through.

For example, he could have very difficult days at work. He's a psychologist with challenging cases. It could get very heavy for him. I quickly understood that he needed twenty minutes to relax and let work go without me jumping on him to chat even though I'd been home alone all day.

We're in similar work situations, so I could understand what he needed and the weight that work could put on our shoulders.

My age (not that I'm very old) helped, I've lived through previous relationships. So, when there were moments that weren't working, I just asked him straight up, "What do you need right now?"

In the end, the things we were worried about didn't happen.

It really helps that even if Jolan isn't necessarily the initiator of the communication, he is always ready to talk. I open the door and he walks through it and together we can say what the other person needs to hear. He could share his concerns without them emotionally affecting me.

For us, there were a few key things that go us through lockdown and our initial period of moving in together:

- Looking out for one another, and in general, being sensitive to the other person's needs.
- Being comfortable being on our own. I had always been independent, not needing to be in a couple to be happy. And he's the same way.
- Verbalizing what we're feeling and what we're going through - and all this in a language that isn't maternal to either of us. Flemish for him, French for me. And we speak English together. Every now and then we would miss a trick because of the language, but we would talk it through until we understood.

In French, we have an expression: *La mayonnaise prend bien.*

If you've ever made mayonnaise, then you know that sometimes, despite all your best efforts, it just doesn't take. And then, other times, it goes smoothly.

That was our case.

We certainly didn't expect lockdown to last for two months. We lived some hard times together too with my grandfather passing, but he was there for me every step. And I didn't expect it. It brought us even more together. I learned that he could also navigate this relationship when things weren't easy.

These are some other things we learned which helped:

- We know ourselves well and what is most important to us individually.
- Finding some space, even if there isn't much, to create some mental space as well. And we were sharing with other housemates! (Which was harder for him than it was for me)
- Communicating everything. Not letting things slip by because even the small things are important. Otherwise, they become big things!
- Not assuming that the guy can figure out what's wrong because it seems evident. We have to say it out loud. Whether it be a question of emotions, needs, sex - whatever the subject, we have to talk about it! We're all different; we have to say it because the answers don't just fall from the sky. Drop the prince charming expectations. The idea that love 'just happens' romantically is bull****! I say what I want and what I need, and then we figure it out. It's so much easier that way. Fairy tales really let us down on that.

- Have a good balance between moments alone and moments together.
- We had great evenings together, and sure we both put on about ten pounds, but we consider them an accessory! We had such fun together – cooking, games, drinking, dressing up, watching cartoons.

While we weren't thinking "This lockdown will make or break us", in fact, that's exactly what happened. The lockdown accelerated our relationship. We were suddenly sharing *all* our moments together when before we'd only had the occasional weekend or a getaway.

Indeed, this was a period of such intensity that it was going to make or break us.

And it made us.

The next thing for us to figure out is how to make our lives come geographically nearer to one another since we've become so much closer emotionally thanks to this lockdown

PART II

WHAT'S HAPPENING TO US? UNDERSTANDING THE IMPACT OF LOCKDOWN

7

Flipping Our Lids: What's happening in our brain

I often talk about this issue with my clients in counseling. We have all experienced times when we just don't see reason, we're not rational, we say things, and sometimes do things that we would never do if we were in 'our right mind'!

Neurobiology is such a complex science; the person who best helped me to understand it (and then in turn I help my clients understand it), was Dr. Dan Siegel. He explains in his book *Mindsight: The New Science of Transformation* (Siegel 2001), and he also has a great YouTube video called "Dr. Dan Siegel presenting a Hand Model of the Brain" (Siegel 2012), which I encourage all partners, parents, and anyone to watch.

I'd like to explain it here, in a nutshell, the way I do when I am counseling people:

Picture your brain as your hand. Hold up your open hand, then fold in your thumb, then fold your four fingers down, over your palm and your thumb. It's like a fist with your thumb inside. There you go – it's your brain!

I'll now explain each of the parts and what they do, and why we react the way we sometimes do with our partners, and then I'll explain why this may be such an issue in lockdown during a pandemic.

Now open your hand again, and here are the parts of the brain.

<u>Wrist</u> – that is your spinal cord, which sends messages between the brain and body

<u>Palm</u> – the brain stem, the oldest part of the brain, which regulates things like our breathing, our heartbeat, our digestion, and where we, when we feel threatened, we have the Fight/Flight/Freeze response

<u>Thumb</u> (folded into our palm) – this works closely with the brain stem and is known as the limbic region, which likely developed 200 million years ago when we became mammals. With the brain stem, it is where we create emotions – fear, anger, sadness, attachment – and also memory is divided up there, in the areas known as the amygdala and hippocampus.

<u>Fingers folded over thumb and palm</u>: this is the cortex, where we make "maps" of the world through sight and sound, where we make associations in thought, and where we regulate attention, language, and imagination among others.

<u>Fingertips</u> – below the last knuckle to our fingernails – is the prefrontal cortex. This is where we have executive functions, like impulse control, control of emotional reactivity, planning and more. It's also where integration between all areas of the brain takes place.

Now fold all your fingers over your thumb. This is what integration looks like. The more integration we have in our brain, the more harmony, connection, and flexibility we have.

Now flip all your fingers up... and you have a brain with less integration. The less integration we have, the more chaos, outbursts, and rigidity we experience. With these fingers up, we have 'flipped our lids'!

Now where do you think we work best with our partners? A rhetorical question, of course. Flipped lids do not help us solve problems or conflicts. They do not help us feel closer and more connected and loving. Flipped lids create frustration, anger, distance, and disharmony.

Now we can see how it works, how the parts of the brain can all work together or apart to create moments in our relationships.

Sure, that is nice, and a bit academic - but what makes us 'flip our lids'? And what are some things we can do about it to close our lid and bring us back into integrated harmony?

That's what really matters during lockdown.

In primitive times we really needed our Brain Stem and our Limbic System to be on the alert. After all, the 'lions, tigers, and bears' (nod to the Wizard of Oz movie) were much bigger, and stronger, fiercer, and more deadly than we were! If we didn't have our warning system to let us know that the lions, tigers, and bears were nearby we'd all be gone now as a species. But with the brain stem and limbic system working together, we knew there was danger, our bodies would flood with hormones like adrenaline and cortisol, and then we would either fight that tiger or flee from that bear.

Obviously, the system worked because we are still here as a species!

But these days it is rare that we would actually be confronted by a lion, a tiger, or a bear. The interesting thing about our protective limbic system and brain stem is that it is such a powerful mechanism for the continuation of the species and individual that even *perceived* threats trigger the Fight/Flight/Freeze response.

For example, our partner may say something to us that reminds us of an upsetting reprimand from the past that a parent said when we were young.

We probably don't even make the connection right away, but there it is. Our brain is triggered - we flip our lid. We feel scared or hurt, or angry. We react with an outburst (angry or tearful perhaps) or run away and don't address our feelings, and we DON'T EVEN KNOW WHY!

But our brain remembers even if we don't consciously.

The good thing is with some self-reflection we can often figure out what the trigger was, and oftentimes we already know some of the things that do trigger us to flip our lids.

But now here's the difficult thing for us to deal with during lockdown...

We are trying to protect ourselves from a deadly virus!

There is an invisible "lion, tiger and bear" out there, and we don't feel safe. We feel threatened, if not all, then much of the time. Just to go outside and live what was once our "normal" life can feel as if we are stepping into apocalyptic times with an invisible enemy. Our baseline for feeling in danger is higher; our brain is more reactive.

So some little thing our partner has done may now seem like a BIG thing. We perceive it as a threat, or we react more intensely than we might ever have done in our past "normal" life.

Our lids flip more easily, more often, more intensely during lockdown, and this is a huge challenge for our loving relationships.

Okay so now, once we have flipped our lids, have had our anger, or tears and now our partner is upset too. What can we do to "re-integrate", to find that peace and harmony of our brain being back un-flipped?

It is amazing how much this simple hand model of the brain has been a helpful tool for my clients and for myself. With this understanding, not only can we take some of our and our partner's irrational behavior out of the realm of criticism and powerlessness, but we can also move back into the realm of understanding and self-forgiveness while moving forward with empowerment to a more peaceful and fulfilling life.

––––––

Activities

1. Deep breathing – breathe our first, then take a deep breath in through the nose, hold for two seconds, then out through the mouth, into the abdomen (you can actually watch your abdomen go in and out). Do this until you feel calmer. It could be as few as 3 breaths, but it could be more depending on the level of upset.

2. Do something physical like taking a walk, a run, a swim, lifting weights, whatever you can do. This also helps the breathing but it also calms the body, which helps to calm the mind.

3. Meditate if that is something you already do, or you could learn to do it. There are many apps available these days.

4. Have a scent handy like an essential oil that you like, so that as soon as you realize you have flipped your lid, you can breathe that in a few times. It seems to have a remarkable effect on settling the brain back down.

5. Watch Dan Siegel's "Hand Model of the Brain" on YouTube (Siegel 2012) to see this model in action.

8

Couples of All Kinds in Lockdown

"Red and yellow and pink and green, purple and orange and blue..." (Shout out to everyone who remembers this song from their childhood... or their children's childhood...)

When I think about the couples I know, even just in my own circle of friends, colleagues, acquaintances, and family, they have one thing in common:

They are all different.

It's been helpful for me to think of couples as a life of their own:

There's Jo.

There's Helen.

There's Jo-and-Helen.

Maybe you've noticed that individual members of a couple act differently when they are with their partners. That's a very concrete illustration of the Jo-and-Helen concept.

Maybe you've noticed it in yourself, that your concerns, your interests, and your ways of communicating are different with your partner than it is in most other relationships in your life. This is normal. It's the Jo-and-Helen concept.

Now, there's an additional layer to this.

There's Jo.

There's Helen.

There's Jo-and-Helen.

There's Jo-and-Helen-in-Lockdown.

It's another being, an entity of its own. And this multiplies for more than just Jo-and-Helen. Anne-and-Jules-in-Lockdown, Mac-and-Steve-in-Lockdown, Amanda-and-Ron-in-Lockdown. And so the list goes on.

The way Jo-and-Helen worked before isn't the way Jo-and-Helen-in-Lockdown operate. Their communication might improve or deteriorate as they move from one version of their couple to another. Their way of relating, the way they spend their time together, and their sex life is going to evolve.

And once again, there's no predictable route the relationships will take. What changes for Jo-and-Helen-in-Lockdown will differ from Mac-and-Steve-in-Lockdown.

This may sound obvious, so...

What's the point of this chapter?

Patience.

Much of this book focuses on our own relationships: how we perceive them, how we grow them, how we simply keep them alive during lockdown.

What's harder to keep front of mind is that every couple we know is going through the same.

A friend called me and said she was struggling. That her husband was being a jerk towards her and treating her like she was a bag of crap. When I asked her to give detail, she mentioned a list of minor infractions like "not emptying the dishwasher after I asked him", "woke me up when he knew I really needed to sleep in", and "constantly making noise".

My first reaction was to tell her how unreasonable she was being, that her expectations were way out of line with what would be small annoyances during regular times, much less during a global pandemic.

Fortunately, I caught myself before saying that out loud.

I asked more questions about how she was feeling in general, what was happening in her family and work since she started working from home.

To sum it up - there was a lot going wrong in my friend's life.

While I first found myself jumping to judgments (How can she talk about him so meanly during a lockdown? How can my normally level-minded friend be so dramatic?) I recognized that I had only one job in the situation.

To listen.

To nod my head (over Zoom).

And perhaps, finally, to offer some small snippets of ideas that might help her be more at ease with her situation.

Her complaints about the relationship were secondary to all the rest happening in her life, where she had some serious problems. She used complaining about her relationship as a way to ease the general stress and pressure she was feeling.

Couples are made up of themselves plus everything happening around them. A pandemic throws a hundred magnifying glasses on each of those otherwise secondary stressors.

I learned in that moment (and continue learning!) about staying curious, asking questions, and helping those close to me come to terms with what's happening in their relationship, just as they do the same for me. Like when my husband was lounging around the house while I was working thirteen-hour online shifts for work.

His mere presence drove me crazy.

I whined and complained about it to my friends, who sympathized while also illuminating me to the fact that my irritation had everything to do with my state of mind and not his behavior... and they did it in the subtle and supportive ways.

"You must be exhausted," they said to me. "I can't even imagine the pressure you're feeling. Your husband is so lucky to have such free time. I'd certainly be jealous of that."

Oh yes, look, that feeling I have about my husband is not irritation, but jealousy. That's something I could talk with him about. And you know what happened when I did?

He started making more dinners and cleaning the toilet.

The toilet!

Thank you, friends.

———

Activity

Two breaths and a sneeze.

That sounds like a funny equation for a chapter about listening, questions, and patience, right?

When someone tells you something about their relationship, and you're tempted to jump in with advice (like me!) take two breaths and then a fake sneeze.

Why?

The two breaths create space. I suggest doing them in a way that the person can hear (on the phone) or see (on Zoom) so that they know you're still engaged. Then you can say:

"One sec, I'm going to sneeze." You don't actually have to sneeze, though I do an amazing fake sneeze and it's become a bit of a party trick.

What does a fake sneeze do?

It interrupts your course of thinking. The path you were on where you had great ideas that you thought the person had to hear - they vacate the premises. You go back to zero.

And you start asking questions. They can be questions that have the person repeat in different words what they've said to you, because sometimes even just the act of repeating brings new ideas to light. Questions could be:

"So what is the exact thing that annoys you?"

"Tell me again how [annoying moment] happened?"

"What do you think is putting you over the edge?"

"When [partner] said [hurtful/annoying thing], how did you feel in the moment? How do you feel now?"

"Do you have any idea why [partner] is behaving that way?"

This is hardly a start. But anytime you're going to take on one of these conversations, consider starting with two breaths and a sneeze to clear the slate.

9

Teasing Apart the Different Stressors

We all have multiple stressors pulling on us during a time of crisis. This is even more acute during a global pandemic when the outcome remains unknown. Regardless of whether or not we have been personally affected in a direct way by the pandemic, all of us have felt the effects.

Self-awareness is an ongoing theme in this book, and so we want to acknowledge here the importance of recognizing each of the different stressors you may be experiencing, and their cumulative impact on your behavior in your relationship.

Below are some questions on specific stressors that may be invading your personal well-being. Naming these stressors helps us recognize which elements are pulling down our individual resilience, which has a pretty immediate impact on our romantic relationships.

Work Stressors

- Is job security creating anxiety for me?
- Am I worried that I won't have enough income to get us through?
- Are my colleagues vying for the promotion that I wanted?
- Has my boss become out of control due to their own stressors? Are they taking it out on me and am I by extension taking it out on others?
- Has my productivity dropped so badly that I think my job may be at risk? Or that I'm violating my own personal standards?
- Have my future prospects been affected by the pandemic or other fallout from it?

Health-related Stressors

- Is the status of the pandemic in my neighborhood/region stressing me out?
- Do I have health problems that could be worsened due to this pandemic? Do I feel I would be well-supported by our health-care system should I fall ill?
- Do I have other health issues that were weighing on me even before all this pandemic stuff happened?
- Do I have loved ones whom I fear could be affected by this health crisis or another?
- Am I experiencing sensations of panic, frustration, anxiety, or depression that I need to address with a professional?

Social Stressors

- Are my relationships with family and friends in the same condition as they were before this crisis? Do I feel like some rebuilding with them needs to happen?
- Do I see enough people to feel socially fulfilled or do I still miss human contact?
- Do I have friends or family going through really difficult times and I'm unable to support them the way I would have in the 'old days'?

Environmental Stressors

- Do I watch too much news? Is it getting me down?
- Does that sight of people wearing masks induce anxiety in me?
- Are crowds gathering in my city? Does that make me nervous?
- When I step into the grocery store, do I see germs everywhere?
- Am I required to take public transit, sometimes crowded, and does this affect me?
- Does human touch by strangers make me recoil in a way it never used to?
- Is my home a safe place to be? Are my neighbors getting on my nerves? Did I have home renos in progress that have been stalled, preventing me from living normally in my home?
- Do the limitations on travel abroad have a direct impact on my lifestyle?

Financial Stressors

- Are expenses stacking up?
- Is my livelihood at risk?
- Am I financially supporting members of my family to the point that it is putting a strain on my financial situation?
- Am I behind on payments?
- Will I need to dip into savings, or have I already come close to using them up?

Family Stressors

- Have I lost loved ones over the course of the past few months? Am I still grieving?
- Are members of my family flipping out? Is this wearing on me?
- Am I far from my family, unable to connect with them the way I'm used to?
- Have members of my family experienced various kinds of setbacks?
- Is there abuse happening in my family that I am not in a position to stop?
- Are members of my family experiencing mental health challenges due to or worsened by the pandemic?
- Children. (I'm just going to leave it at that since children are not the focus of this book and we could write volumes about this subject alone!)

The list above demonstrates just how much is pulling at us before we even begin to consider the stressors of our romantic relationship!

...and as you'll have noticed, it's not exhaustive. I'm sure as you read these, you added your own stressors to the list.

No wonder our relationships are also a challenge.

We bring a lot into the room when we are with our partners. When something our partner says or does sets us off, there are inevitably other stressors affecting our reaction.

————

Questions for Reflection

Am I experiencing some stressors that I can start taking action on right now?

How can naming my other stressors during 'downtime' with my partner help them to see the full list of things I'm dealing with?

...Is my partner experiencing stressors that I don't see? How can I ask my partner in a supportive way to share with me all the stressors they are facing now?

When I'm frustrated with my partner, are other stressors magnifying my feelings? Can I tease those other stressors away so that I deal with the issue at hand and not multiple stressors at once?

10

'Hot Potato' Topics

In every relationship, there are a few topics that are just too 'hot' to handle.

When confronted with these, one or the other or both partners get so heated about the issue that they seem to 'flip their lids' (see the chapter on this subject) every time the topic is discussed, even though they set out to deal with it in a very reasonable and rational way.

The intention is positive, but the topic is so rooted in emotion for some reason, either for one or both partners, that agreement just cannot be reached. The topic can never seem to be discussed in a calm, rational way to get to a solution.

As also mentioned throughout this book, there is no shame in going for professional help on these issues. You have tried over and over to come to a solution on these 'hot potato' topics, but both of you end up angry or frustrated or hurt over and over and over again, no matter how hard you try to resolve it.

While there may be any number of issues that can be 'hot potato' topics, we have found in couple counseling they often fall into three basic categories:

Intimacy (or sex), Finances, and In-Laws

Probably no surprises there!

In each of these often is a question of 'not enough':

- Not enough sex, or closeness or affection. One partner may need to feel closeness before feeling sexual desire. The other partner may need to have physical sexual contact in order to feel close!

- Not enough money. Not enough to meet the basic needs of the family. Or sometimes it is not enough to meet what we *think* are our needs, when really there is an underlying belief that material items are signs of success. In lockdown, many people's incomes were greatly reduced or lost completely, and the stress on the couple was magnified even more.

- Not enough support from our partners regarding our in-laws – their family. In an ideal world, we would all get along with each other's families, but it just isn't an ideal world. We may feel unsupported by our partner. They may feel in the middle between their partner and their families.

Under 'normal' life circumstances these issues can be difficult enough to deal with, but in lockdown, they may rear their heads even more than usual. These kinds of issues are tough so, again, don't be afraid to seek help if you cannot come to a satisfactory resolution together.

I suppose this chapter may sound like a plug for counseling, and I guess it is! After all, as a couple, isn't our goal to have a satisfying, cooperative, richly loving journey through life together?

11

A Lockdown Love Story:
What now?

My husband and I live in Southern France. He's French, I'm not. We've been married for three years and have a gorgeous golden retriever. The sea is just 'over there' from where we live in one of the Mediterranean cities. It's walkable, but not see-able from our large-on-French-standards-but-small-on-North-American-standards apartment. We have two balconies. Paint is falling off the walls, every tap drips, the wallpaper is a mishmash of fake wood and sparkly linen (which apparently is a thing) and hasn't been updated in at least twenty-odd years. Such is the rental life in France. But we're happy here.

In his day job, my husband is a trainer. In my day job, I'm helping an international children's charity prevent its workers from abusing or exploiting children. Heavy stuff.

We're on our own (with the golden retriever) though we have plans to build our family. For now, we are trying to make the most of our lazy Sunday mornings, since we understand those are the first to go with parenthood.

When talk of the virus first began, we knew something was coming our way. My hubby is originally a biologist (a virologist, to be specific, aka working on viruses) and spoke about the history of epidemics. I've witnessed tragedies like Ebola and cholera from up close through my work in countries that struggled to respond to the outbreaks.

So when I had to travel for work in February 2020 to Bangkok, I wore my mask on the plane. I started wearing a mask while traveling in 2012 because, simply, I discovered that I didn't get sick anymore. There's a lot of germ-junk in the air, especially while flying. I've long been a fan of my woolen mask. I didn't really fear the coronavirus at that time, but I figured the mask wouldn't hurt.

When I returned home to France, my mother (co-author of this book - more on her later) called me and said, "I think we have to cancel our trip to see you in March." And that's when I started really watching what was happening around us. Mom is older (exact age not to be revealed) and has asthma. Her partner has diabetes. I have asthma. Hubby is fit as a mule.

But I started to worry.

I've been in lockdown before, and this time there were small signs of it coming (not the least the media saying they thought it's coming). Then Friday the thirteenth of March hit (dunh, dunh, dunh = scary music) and I got this sneaking suspicion that things were going to get tough. I thought, "I've gotta go shopping!"

In our pantry, we had a bag of spaghetti and two cans of corn. Definitely not enough to get us through a couple of weeks.

I took my wheelie grandma shopping bag (I love that thing) and headed to the relatively busy but not yet zombie-apocalypse-style grocery store.

As I was picking up cans of beans and jars of sauce and a very reasonable amount of toilet paper, I got a phone call from my staff member resigning as she had to relocate with her kids. Then I received a notification that Air France flights were being canceled. Then I got an email from the health department warning me that because I have asthma I had to take extra precautions.

Friday, March 13th, 2020.

On March 17th, my husband's birthday, we were in full lockdown. On March 19th, my birthday, we were scheduled to buy a house. We didn't.

Grocery stores were open, as well as newspaper stands (because some people here still read them), and bakers (because... well, croissants) but pretty much everything else was closed, closed, closed.

We were allowed out once a day for one hour (and to let the dog do her business). When we went out, we had to carry a specific government form indicating our reason for going out, the date, the time, and a signature.

People asked to borrow our dog to take her for a walk.

I prepared the kitchen for long-term cooking from cans.

On that first night of lockdown, we applauded, along with most of France, at 8 pm for health workers. We then settled in for a movie.

We didn't know what was coming. Numbers on the news weren't helpful because we didn't know actual numbers of cases. Italy, our neighbor and only a few hours away by train, was a mess. A complete mess with horror stories of people dying on stretchers in hallways. I tried to erase those images from my mind. Italy is close. Really close.

We made predictions. We made plans. We had ideas. And a lot of the time we tried to pretend that everything was normal.

We watched the news as all our plans for the coming weeks - and months - started to fade before us. What would happen now?

My husband put his arm around me. Normally we're both really chatty, a couple who never runs out of things to say. But that night, we had no words. I leaned in against his shoulder and found my mind stuck on the idea of *what if...* And that's what led to the next chapter, Building a Contingency Plan.

12

Careful Now: Building a contingency plan

My husband and I tried to talk about what we would do if one of us were to get sick.

The problem is that he is able to think about things in the abstract, whereas I am definitely not. I go straight to imagining it happening and in some ways, I actually live it in the moment. In many situations, this difference in approach is a real benefit to our couple. But there are times - like this one - that it really didn't serve us well. He was considering the implications of wills, mortgages, and next of kin, while I was doing everything in my power to hold back a rush of tears.

Finally, he said, "But what is there to worry about?"

To which I replied, "How about you lying dead on a gurney? How about me watching you die of some unknown disease? What about living the rest of my life without you? That's what I'm worried about!"

Cue: Rush of tears.

The conversation was a total mess. We couldn't advance, though we were doing our best. I just couldn't remove myself emotionally from the topic. Even though I really *wanted* a contingency plan, doing it our normal way of chatting about it over the dinner table just wasn't going to work.

We had to take a few steps back. We had to recognize that both of us needed to be in a certain state of mind for us to be able to have this conversation. And that even then, it might be a conversation we simply couldn't have.

But we both knew that having a plan was important and we had to find a way to be able to talk about the scary 'What Ifs'.

Instead, we broke it up into bite-size chunks.

We exchanged emails on specific topics from our separate home offices down the hall from each other. In that way, little by little, we built a contingency plan, which, I am very thankful to be able to say, so far we haven't needed.

————

Activity

Are you the type who likes to have a plan in place? Maybe you are more the type who prefers to live in the moment?

Building a contingency plan can be a very emotionally charged activity. But if you are a planner that a part of you will feel unfinished until your contingency plan is in place.

While one partner alone *can* develop a contingency plan, really this is an opportunity as a couple to better understand each other's wishes.

While some couples may be able to handle the conversation over dinner, others will find themselves too emotionally involved for an informal conversation (see story above).

Here are some ways you can build a contingency plan if you are a mixed planning/non-planning couple:

- Use an online collaboration tool like Google Docs to have headers that then each person can add bullet points to underneath which expresses either their personal wishes or how they think certain communal aspects should be handled. (I suggest setting a date by which this will be done, or else it might never be done...)
- Start an email chain in which you pose specific, and bite-size questions for your partner to answer, while providing your own answers within.
- Have a stack of sticky notes and a single piece of paper with one heading on each. Watch a movie together and scratch down ideas onto the sticky notes, affixing them to the appropriate page, over the course of the film. Then, the person who is the planner, and type them up and share it with the partner.

Bear in mind, if you are a planner and your partner is not, this could be a very undesirable activity for your partner. Having a large document with a deadline that is far off is likely to result in non-completion and more frustration. While breaking things up into smaller pieces can make it more manageable, the sensation that the activity is dragging on will also be uncomfortable for your live-in-the-moment partner.

Together, negotiate the best way to produce your plan.

———

Resources

Do an online search for "emergency plan". There are many now which are pandemic-related. But consider looking at other types of emergency plans that are suitable for your family's situation.

13

Triggers

So this was a fun list to prepare.

Look, there is a lot of information available online about emotional triggers in a way that is at least as effective as we could cover here. Run a simple Google search and a multitude of quality resources will appear. So rather than reiterating advice and insight you can find online, here are some of the triggers that people reported as emotional triggers during the period of lockdown.

It goes a little something like this:

"My partner..."

- refused to stop stealing the bed sheets, knowing that I slept badly without it.
- asked me how I was feeling when I had just returned from a shopping trip, which always makes me super anxious.
- didn't ask me how I was feeling (not from the same

person, or else that partner really would never be able to get it right).

- played balalaika at midnight (yes, that one was me).
- insisted on frying onions that we never ate, the waste just kills me.
- commented non-stop on my use of a CPAP machine.
- waited until I washed dishes. I can't stand those old gender stereotypes.
- laid on the sofa all day, just like my father used to do.
- whenever asking for something, would say the words "Can you just". Can you just make me a coffee, can you just move while I reorganize the office, can you just whip something easy for dinner, can you just be happy with what I made for dinner. If I hear the words "Can you just..." one more time, I'm just going to lose it!
- wouldn't let the baby cry out, which was what we planned. In fact, every decision we had made as a couple was wasted time. My partner did whatever they wanted anyway.

Some specific words that came up as triggers were:

- Any swear words (various forms of f*** coming up most often)
- "I've told you a million times..."
- "I can't"
- Any reference to what other couples were doing
- Saying no without explaining why
- "You're being so ___."
- "You never ___."
- "That's ridiculous."
- "Later, not now."
- "You always..."

When we are "triggered," we often feel disempowered, hence the anger, frustration, and sometimes tears. It is as if we are at the mercy of the trigger and the person who (perhaps inadvertently) "triggered" us.

But there is power in how we think about things, and even this language is a bit backward.

Rather than saying or thinking: "You triggered me", it is more empowering to say "I am triggered by..."

We put the locus of control back into our own hands so to speak. Once we realize that this trigger is internal to us, we can start to identify it and to understand its impact on us, and WHY it is so impactful. Then our work, either on our own or with our partner, or even with the help of a professional, is to recognize it, name it, discern its origins, and find ways that help defuse the trigger.

We very likely never lose our triggers altogether, but we can find ways to deal with them when they occur so that we feel less disempowered and more in control, safe, and empowered. Some of this is addressed in our chapter on What is going on in the brain: Flipping our lids.

Literature and counseling will tell you much more, but the keys to dealing with triggers are basically three-fold:

1. Knowing they exist.

Not pretending they don't. Identifying them when they happen and noting the nature of the emotional reaction that follows (anger, frustration, despair, etc.)

2. Recognizing that the other person most likely didn't intend to trigger us.

While there might be some exceptions, in the vast majority of healthy relationships, a partner is not aiming to switch a trigger (and especially not during a lockdown situation). They may or may not even know such a trigger exists.

3. As much as possible, pausing before reacting when a trigger is switched.

Getting curious about it, being able to communicate with our partner that a trigger has occurred.

Triggers will happen during lockdown and after - they are a part of our life and often stem from past treatment or experiences, even if we cannot identify exactly how (see the chapter on Family Cultures). Like most emotional experiences, they are heightened during periods of crisis, such as a lockdown or a global pandemic.

14

Compassion for Self and Others

The chicken and the egg.

We often hear that we cannot love someone else unless we are able to love ourselves.

However, I have seen many couples who truly do love one another, and yet have self-esteem, self-worth, or even self-love deficits.

These issues often come out more in conflict or power struggles with one another and are not necessarily an indication of mutual love.

So the issues of compassion and self-compassion are similar. One definition of compassion is the "sympathetic consciousness of others' distress together with a desire to alleviate it" (Merriam-Webster online Dictionary). Clearly, two elements are central: the awareness of others' pain and suffering AND a desire to take some action to help!

We can take this concept even further, into the social sphere. The great physician and psychotherapist, Dr. Alfred Adler, referred to this in German as "Gemeinshaftsgefuhl" (Adler 2011) – having a feeling for the other, caring about the other, doing for the other, and another translation often used is "social interest" or altruism (to give without expecting in return).

Both compassion and social interest taken to the next level is *empathy*: walking in the footsteps of the other, seeing with the eyes of the other, and feeling with the heart of the other (Adler 1930).

We can see how compassion (and empathy) can be a way to closely connect with our loved one. Imagine if our partner were simply to say: "I don't know exactly what you are going through because it has never happened to me, but you must feel so...sad...lonely...grieving.... frustrated. Is there anything I can do? I am here for you, whatever will help you."

Imagine... It sounds wonderful, doesn't it? Often it is not so much that our partner is not feeling that way, but rather that our partner simply does not know how to express that deep feeling of compassion for what we are going through, and vice versa. (Please see the chapter on listening with your heart).

In the pandemic, when emotions, fears, frustrations, sorrows are running even higher, imagine the comfort we would feel knowing how connected our partner is to us, and we to them because we find ways to communicate that understanding to one another.

When it comes to self-compassion, however, it can be much more difficult. Who is the harshest judge of ourselves? WE are! Who expects excellence, greatness, and even perfection of ourselves? WE do!

So while we may be able to be understanding, and compassionate, and even empathic of our loved one, we may be the last person to do that for ourselves!

Again, imagine what comfort it would be if we were able to tell ourselves "I am a human being. I am not an infinite being. I am not perfect, nor can I be! But I am a good person, even with my faults."

Being self-compassionate means being accepting, loving, and honoring of our imperfect humanity (Neff 2011). Another concept, that of 'having the courage to be imperfect' (Dreikurs 1957), is a part of that self-compassion.

Compassion means not focusing on the negative, not judging others harshly for being imperfect, for making mistakes, but rather treating them with kindness and understanding.

Imagine if we did this for ourselves. Imagine how freeing that would be, for us to support ourselves in our frail humanity. Imagine how we could then connect even more with those whom we love on a more open, accepting, unconditionally loving level.

In lockdown, we are not only more often face to face with our partners, but also with that person who looks back at us from the mirror.

We are more stressed and on edge.

We are fighting the invisible enemy of COVID-19.

We may not want to be super creative or productive or innovative.

We may need to lay low. Or we may need to keep busy.

Whatever may be our state of mind, our higher level of stress can put us in a position where we are more aware of our faults and failings. We may be less forgiving and understanding of ourselves than usual. Of course, this will only add to the tensions, the pressures on the limbic brain (as discussed in the chapter on the brain). In the end, we just feel worse, and worse and worse.

So what does come first, compassion or self-compassion?

Often it is compassion, as we are often more readily willing to understand and accept and not judge others but then we may stop there. I implore you NOT to stop there, but to apply your kindness, your understanding, your caring, your desire to assist others... *to yourself*. Your life will be more fulfilling, more easeful, and more loving, in the pandemic and out!

15

A Lockdown Love Story: It sucked

I called my son, crying. I felt so alone and like I was going crazy. I hated the lockdown. The university where I work had closed and I had been stuck at home for months. I missed seeing my friends, greeting colleagues, chatting with students, leading my team, having talks about small and big things and laughing at jokes. I missed it all.

My husband's work didn't close and so when he left for the day, it was just me and our blind 16-year-old dog in the house. All day long. It was one big drag. I thought, *this sucks*, more often than I can count. When he came home, I was all over him like white on rice.

I cleaned. I cooked. I cleaned some more. I watched some movies and a few Netflix series. However, as someone who is used to being on her feet and moving around all day, I just couldn't sit down and watch eight hours of TV. It's just not me. I did some painting and completed some work we needed to do in the basement. I organized EVERYTHING.

There were some things that helped. I started doing a Zoom exercise class with a friend. Once we could create our 'bubbles' we also started seeing our beloved grandkids on the weekends. Playing with them again brought us some of the joy that had been missing.

But during the weekdays, I was mostly miserable. After four months, I just could not take it anymore. I called my son and cried, telling him how horrible I felt. He reassured me; but the thing is nobody knows what will happen and how long this is going to last. It's frustrating and it makes me sad.

Finally, when we could leave the house, I began a walking routine with a friend with a lot of space between us. This really helped my mental state. I found myself relaxing and I really enjoyed our talks. My daughter called a lot more too, and I looked forward to our weekly catch ups. Things were looking up.

Work just called me the other day and asked me to return. Since only so few students are back on campus, they only need a handful of us. I am thrilled to have been selected and I jumped at the chance. Now I'm back at work and feeling like myself again.

I think the lockdown is much harder for social people like me. My husband can stay in the house with just me and be as happy as a clam. But I need my social time and my girl time. It's part of who I am. He is a good support and lets me vent, so that is nice.

After 43 years of marriage, we are still very happy together. However, I, myself, was not happy with being stuck inside alone.

I really hope everything is back to normal soon. We've all been through a lot. I know that some people have had it a lot worse than us - they have lost their jobs or maybe they won't be able to find anything when the lockdown is over. I know we are blessed. But it was a really hard time being by myself for most of the day.

The lockdown? In two words: it sucked.

16

Cultures: International

Do you and your partner come from different cultural backgrounds?

Each of us writing this book is in an international relationship. While it wasn't a prerequisite for being an author on this book, it has likely colored our perspective in ways we don't even recognize.

Here's the thing about being in an international couple, which many of you are probably already aware of:

You cannot take anything for granted.

Words. Physical gestures. Non-verbal cues. Tones of voice. Humor.

The list goes on. The aspects of communication that we've grown up taking for granted are in many ways invalid. We have to start at zero (or maybe at, like, five out of a hundred) when understanding our partner-of-another-land.

In lockdown, our physical worlds get smaller; so do our perspectives. It's inevitable. We've already talked in other points in this book about the volume of change we experience during the time of a global pandemic, and this change forces us to hold onto those fewer aspects of life that we perceive as ultimate truths.

But ultimate truths are wildly dependent on the culture in which we were born.

There's another layer of this, in the culture of our family, but that's covered in the next chapter.

Here let's talk about world cultures that come under a magnifying glass in our couple.

If you are in an international couple, certainly you've already come across some of these challenges:

• Partner A makes a joke; Partner B is offended

• Partner C comments on the family of Partner D; Partner D explodes at the perceived insensitivity of Partner C

• Partner E closes the door to their home office and won't come out; Partner F feels isolated even though Partner E insists nothing is wrong

• Partner G makes political comments at a party; Partner H is horrified

SPOILER ALERT: You could just as easily see this same list in the next chapter. These behaviors are not so unusual and definitely aren't specific to international couples. However, the reason behind them can make the difference in how we address them.

Here we'll focus on a few of the international culture issues that lead to these rifts.

1. Language
2. High versus Low Context
3. Assumptions

Language

My native language is English. My husband is French. His English is perfect, but his accent is most decidedly foreign. My French is very good, but most people in France assume I'm German or English or Albanian (that last one only happened once). We're pretty lucky in having strong language skills between us where we can generally understand each other's intentions and humor... with some big exceptions.

When he makes a joke in French - forget it, I just don't even understand the words.

On top of that, my husband learned English in the UK. Therefore, his humor in English is British. I'm Canadian. Many think that would mean I have a similar sense of humor to the Brits.

I don't.

My husband will say things in the exact same voice and exact same face that he says serious things, then I will blow up at his insensitivity, and then he'll say he was joking. Couldn't I tell?

No. I couldn't. It plays out like this:

Me: J. says we can't bring the dog to her house.

Him: Tell J. she's being ridiculous.

Me: What? I will do no such thing! I hardly even know her and it's totally reasonable that she doesn't want our giant, drooling dog in her home.

Him: No, look at the poor dog. J.'s being ridiculous.

Me: You want me to ruin my friendship with J. before I even know her by calling her ridiculous? *"Tu es ridicule"*? That's what you want me to say?

Him: Not at all! I'm joking.

Me: What's joking about that?

Him: Ridiculous and ridicule are not the same thing.

Me: Actually, they are. What did you mean?

Him: It was just a little joke.

Me: A little joke? Did you mean to say she's being silly?

Him: Maybe I meant to say silly.

Me: There's a big difference between ridiculous and silly.

Him: It was just a joke.

And that was a conversation that took place when we weren't even yet in lockdown (it was the week prior).

In lockdown, it would have looked something like this:

Me: J. says when lockdown is finished we should come over, but we can't bring the dog.

Him: Well, that's ridiculous. She has a giant yard and a dog. She's being ridiculous. Tell her she's ridiculous.

Me: You're the one who's ridiculous! How can you be so insensitive! I can't believe you're already putting our new friendship in danger because you don't want to leave the dog behind for a few hours!

Him: You're overreacting! Stop yelling!

Me: You're yelling!

And it would degenerate from there some more.

Words, when even the same words seemingly used in the same context, can be extremely dangerous during lockdown. When speaking in a second (or third or fourth) language, words cannot be taken at face value.

We cannot jump to an immediate judgment or belief from the words our partner says. We have to explore them. A technique (two breaths and a sneeze) mentioned elsewhere in the chapter called "Couples of All Kinds in Lockdown" can also help us to build in some space before reacting to our partner's words. These words may or may not be the words they intended, and they may or may not carry the intent they intended.

Words are dangerous in a multilingual relationship and must be handled lightly.

High versus Low Context

High Context cultures are those where small actions carry big significance. Low Context cultures are those where there is a broader meaning applied to certain words or actions, which means a lower degree of intensity in meaning.

Lower context cultures tend to be more direct, bypassing the importance of facial expressions, gestures, or other cues. There is a lot of literature about this which can be found with a quick online search.

The degree to which high or low context impacts a relationship depends on the individuals within the relationship. Someone might come from a very high context culture - for example, Japan - but have lived most of their adult life in the United States, which is a well-known low context culture.

Culture, just like the people within it, is not fixed.

Being aware of where our partner's culture sits on the high-to-low spectrum can help us identify and discuss non-verbal cues that we might be missing. I live full-time in France, I love French culture and I love my Frenchman - but I am still constantly learning about signs that are otherwise well-known here that I've been missing ever since I arrived.

For example, my French friends love to talk about hot-button issues. Politics, religion, the latest scandal in the Elysée, and the environment.

But when I brought up the topic of laïcité - the separation of religion and state - I had no idea what I was getting into.

Some of my relationships are still recovering from it. That was a conversation I wouldn't have hesitated to have with my friends in Canada or the US or even the UK who are on another part of the spectrum towards high context, but still could handle the topic.

Here, it was a no-go.

Fortunately, I'm in a group of friends who give me a long leash given my own cultural background (and they know I would never say anything with the intention of offending, which is generally a pretty Canadian quality). So my friends have remained my friends.

In a romantic relationship, the intensity of feelings is magnified, so knowing these hot-button issues and being ready to let them go - ESPECIALLY DURING LOCKDOWN - is essential for our mixed low-high context cultural relationships to survive in good health.

Assumptions

Without going into this too much here, as it plays an even larger role in the chapter about family culture, it's none the less important for us to recognize that we live based on assumptions.

I assume my husband knows I'm upset because I'm sullen when I'm normally bubbly. He assumes I'm not hungry because I ate lunch several hours earlier, so even though he's responsible for dinner tonight, he'll serve it when he's ready to do so. These are the daily assumptions of our lives.

And they serve a great purpose!

If we have to question every single little action we ever take, we'll be in decision paralysis. Many of us struggle enough with decisions as it is.

When our relationships cross-cultural borders, our assumptions risk being even less accurate.

Here is a light-hearted example that has played heavily into my Canadian/French relationship.

French people eat breakfast, lunch, and dinner at (generally) set times.

- Breakfast is a croissant/baguette/cookies and coffee/hot chocolate.
- Lunch is some variety of something big.
- Dinner is also big, but sometimes on the lighter end (and if you're visiting in-laws, you never know what to expect - dinner could be a bowl of soup or a three-course smorgasbord).

Canadian people do not have a set way of eating; everyone is different.

As for me, I eat when I'm hungry. My approach is in direct opposition to the French way.

- For breakfast, I like eggs and yogurt.
- For lunch, I usually eat at my computer while working - a big no-no here!
- For dinner, I'm more easy-going but it has to be before 8 pm or else I have nightmares. This fact is met with grimaces and scorn and makes me a terrible dinner guest when people like to eat at 8 or 9 pm.

In lockdown, I am even more erratic. Frankly, I was sick of eating. It was like every meal was another opportunity to see how little things were changing. The Groundhog Day syndrome (If you haven't seen the movie "Groundhog Day", watch it! Watch it now!) This added an emotional intensity to mealtimes (as my husband likes for us to eat together, which I find generally hard to argue with) that we had never before seen as a couple.

Most of our arguments happened over dinner.

My husband assumed that dinner in lockdown was like any other dinner, as dinner in France is a constant, regardless of the external surroundings. Lockdown or not.

For me, dinner had become a symbol of everything I couldn't do, couldn't have, and couldn't be.

Our cultures create excitement, making each day something different, but we have to be ever conscious – even more so in lockdown – when these powerful cultures are the basis of misunderstanding in our relationship.

———

Resource: The Culture Map by Erin Meyer. Her website also has a slew of awesome resources: www.erinmeyer.com

17

Cultures: Family

Regardless of the nature of the family in which you grew up (biological parents or not, extended family, blended family, etc.), a perhaps-surprising element is likely the strongest influencer in defining the kind of relationships we would have.

We "inherit" behavior from those who raised us.

The models of relationships we witnessed as children have colored most aspects of the way we operate now. We may have intentionally tried to be different from those relationships, or tried to emulate them, or we may be like them, without even consciously realizing it.

Families, like couples, come in more than 101 different flavors.

It's not about DNA here; it's about those powerful models we watched day in and day out. That environment impacted the way we grew into adults and ultimately into couples.

I remember once talking with a wise, much older friend about the pitfalls of a relationship I was in at the time. It was not an unhealthy relationship, but ultimately I wasn't getting from it what I was looking for.

But I couldn't figure out what it was that I was looking for.

It was a good relationship. He was a nice guy. He was good to his mother. We had similar interests. But ultimately the way that we related to one another was foreign to me, completely different from the family in which I grew up. So different from how my parents related to each other. I won't idealize my parents' marriage, but certainly what I saw in them - the good that I took away from it - was two people who were able to talk through their issues. They didn't shy away from the difficult conversations. In fact, they brought us all together as a family to resolve together some of the little bumps that may have ultimately one day become big bumps in the family.

And certainly, what was always clear, was the unconditional love that existed in our household.

I realized that was where my relationship was going wrong at the time. It was so reliant upon specific conditions. It relied on us both working. That we had active social lives. Possibly the most destructive characteristic of our relationship came when we had problems – we simply did not talk about them.

That last point was very important for the smooth running of our relationship. Something wrong? Sweep it under the rug. Feeling blue? Paint on a smile or risk being chastised or labeled as a whiner.

What a relief it was to recognize that while our relationship was not inherently unhealthy, we had habits and ways of operating that were too divergent from the very relationship that I wanted to emulate.

Generally speaking, there is no right or wrong when it comes to family culture (assuming it isn't destructive). We choose what we want to bring forward with us. I think most of us have aspects of the family we grew up with that we want to take along for the rest of our lives.

And other parts, we are happy to leave behind.

Modeling by parents is a powerful influence on children. Modeling by caregivers, guardians, adult friends, or other influencers also impacts the judgments we place on relationships and what we're looking for from a partner.

You'll probably have noticed that there's a theme in this book about naming things. That's because so often we can't address an issue until we can call it something. Until we have a name for it, it stays in this ethereal land of the unnamed. It's a vast place at times desolate, and it at times decorated in gold filament with all the detail of a Baroque Catholic Church. There are times when the unnamed serves us specifically because it is unnamed, particularly when it is protecting us from something damaging or hurtful.

However, in the wake of a global pandemic, as we are trying to keep our romantic relationship alive, those unnamed aspects of family culture can sneak up and bite us without us ever really knowing what it was.

That's why it's so important to have a name for "it".

There's a reason why Stephen King's novel called "It" was so powerful, the "It" did not have a name. It simply was.

Sidebar - that book terrified me in my early teens. How did my parents ever let me read it? Oh wait, maybe I saw the movie, yes, now I remember it was at Kim's house during a sleepover in her basement with three other friends and we all had nightmares; none of us slept afterward. I don't think we ever had a sleepover again after that. Oh wait, that wasn't Stephen King's "It", it was the movie "Child's Play". The early 90s were full of hard-core horror movies, weren't they? That murderous doll did a number on the psyches of many in my generation, anyway.

Back to the subject at hand: family cultures.

We need to be able to name our family culture. Maybe you have already done a lot of thinking about your upbringing and about the models of relationships you had. This is often true, especially for those who did not like what they witnessed.

Can you bring that thinking into your relationship in a way that is constructive? Something to be careful about is the risk that we start seeing that named thing everywhere.

So, there is a two-fold opportunity here.

Number one, naming the aspects of the family culture we had when we were young that we want to avoid or keep.

Number two, recognizing that this relationship we're in is not the same one that we witnessed while growing up. No one is ever trying to be like our father or trying to be like that particular role model we had. Or maybe we sought our partner out specifically because they have certain qualities that remind us of an important figure from our youth.

Certainly when my husband is singing "If I Were a Rich Man" in French in the shower, I can't help but have flashbacks to my father singing that song in the basement at three in the morning on his twelve-string guitar. The result is that sometimes I know I am projecting onto my husband certain characteristics that my father had which are only mildly represented in my husband's behavior. My husband cannot possibly know this. He does not know that I'm thinking it, nor that there is such a comparison, since my husband never was able to meet him before my father passed away.

So it's *my* job to recognize it, to call it out, to file it, and to communicate about it when the behavior by my husband is one that triggers me.

———

Questions for Reflection

What behaviors do I see in my partner that remind me of previous role models?

When I am triggered by my partner's behavior because it resembles past models, am I able to identify that sensation and communicate it in a way that is helpful?

Am I able to take time away when I am feeling this kind of negative triggering?

What assumptions do I have about my partner's behavior that may stem from the family culture in which I grew up, and not from my partner's intentions?

What behaviors am I repeating that are not helping my relationship become stronger? Are they around communication? Stress management? Affection? Or something else entirely?

PART III

WHO ARE WE ANYWAY? DIFFERENT WAYS OF BEING IN AND OUT OF LOCKDOWN

18

Introverts & Extroverts

The best explanation of introverts and extroverts I've ever heard is the following. Imagine two clear cups that can each hold a gallon of water. One is filled nearly to the brim. The other is half full. You pour another half-gallon of water into each one. They both fill up. However, one flows over, while the other one does not.

The introvert is the cup that flows over – it just takes a bit of stimulation for the experience to become overwhelming (to overflow). The extrovert on the other hand, appreciates the additional input and feels very good. Their energy level goes up but they do not feel overwhelmed. In fact, they feel better.

When introverts and extroverts get together it can look something like this:

- The extrovert wants to have friends over while the other would rather have a quiet evening.
- The extrovert enjoys parties, meeting people, talking, being gregarious with everyone. The introvert prefers

small gatherings, and if compelled to go to a big party, is likely to converse with one or two people the entire time.

- The extrovert feels better after a social event. The introvert feels drained.
- The introvert needs a lot of alone time to recuperate and recharge. The extrovert needs to be around friends and family, to hang out, to be in social situations.

You get the picture.

It might take a while to adjust to each other's needs and ways of being. However, there is nothing stopping extroverts and introverts from having wonderful, healthy and lasting relationships.

The question is does it get harder or easier for such a couple during lockdown?

Well it depends.

In many ways, lockdown is an introvert's dream. Parties and get-togethers are forbidden and everyone needs to confine in place. There are no social obligations and thus, no need to try to avoid them.

On the other hand, in particular with prolonged confinement, extroverts can feel restless, frustrated, and even sad. Even though they are with their partner, they miss their friends, the get-togethers, the conversations and personal connections, and sharing time and experiences with others. While technology helps, the experience is not the same as being there in person.

If two extroverts are in lockdown together, they will most likely do a lot of things together and it might pose less of an issue.

The same with two introverts – each one in their own space and taking the time they need to do internal processing. However, a couple that are one of each may face some challenges.

So what can you do if you find that you are an extrovert in lockdown with an introvert as a partner?

1. Respect their alone time without needing to be with them all the time
2. Call and video call with family and friends
3. Set up social events online like virtual dance parties, games, and dinners
4. Learn to spend time alone and appreciate some of the positive aspects of that experience
5. Use the time to take a course or learn something to keep occupied and reduce the feeling of missing out
6. Be social with your partner in a way that feels great to both of you. Watching movies, doing a puzzle, listening to music are just a few ideas
7. Exercise to manage the stress of feeling lonely or sad
8. Try meditation and/or yoga to feel better

If you're an introvert confined with an extrovert, you can try:

1. Exercising, meditating, and yoga to recharge yourself
2. Reading or watching films by yourself
3. Journaling your ideas and thoughts in a little quiet corner
4. Giving more together time with your partner to support them during lockdown
5. Participating in games or virtual social events that might seem silly to you but are important to your partner

6. Being together apart; for instance, you can be in the same space and read a book while your partner works on a puzzle or listens to music.

7. Take up a hobby where you can lose yourself like knitting or painting

8. Breathe deeply

————

Activity

Take a questionnaire to find out which type you are, if it isn't already clear. There are a million personality tests online that get at this personality dimension, the most famous one being the Myers Briggs test which you can do for free on www. 16personalities.com (and you even get your own personality avatar!).

Then each of you make a priority list of activities and alone/shared times that are important. These should be respected.

See if there are activities or times that you are more willing to negotiate.

————

Questions for Reflection

Who is an extrovert and who is an introvert in our relationship?

What needs for space and social time do we each have?

What social and alone aspects are important for each of us during confinement?

Can I be a bit more social during this time for my partner?

Can I be a bit less social during this time for my partner?

How will we begin to be social once lockdown ends so that my introvert partner does not feel overwhelmed?

19

Loving Unconditionally:
Unconditional positive regard

So much of our lives are based on our last success – our last job review, our last sale, our last mark at school. As we grow up we often get a sense that our value is based primarily, if not solely, on our actions. If we succeed we are good, worthy, lovable. If we fail, then we are bad, unworthy, unlovable.

As adults, when we look at that construct, it's much easier to recognize that this isn't true. But we are learning these beliefs as children, when 'black & white, 'all or nothing' thinking is the way we do think and assess our experiences.

As adults, while logically we know this doesn't make sense, we may still be carrying some of these messages and beliefs with us without realizing it.

Let us look at these statements above again:

I am lovable, worthy, good, successful, if I …
or when I ….
or because I ….

And then the opposite:

> I am not lovable, worthy, good, successful if I...
> when I...
> or because I...

The first set of statements are known as 'Conditional Positive Regard '– we see ourselves in a positive light conditional upon only our behavior. Basically, we ARE good only if we DO good. In the second set of statements the opposite belief is true – if we DO something "bad" we ARE bad, which is 'Conditional Negative Regard'.

The beauty of **Unconditional** Positive Regard (Rogers 1961, 1967, 1977) is that when we apply it to ourselves, we have more self-worth. With that, we can move into an even closer relationship with our partner.

In an intimate relationship, we may judge our partners this way as well, often without realizing it. As we do it to ourselves, they do it to themselves, and they do it to us. We don't realize how discouraging this can actually be, because who *can* do their best all the time, who *is* perfect? (No one.)

We need to ask ourselves: do we love our partner because of what they DO or because of who they ARE?

Obviously, if they are a kind person, they will do kind deeds, but people who are unkind as people can also do kind deeds. What is at the heart of a person is *who* we love, and this is 'Unconditional Positive Regard'.

We love them whether or not they make mistakes, choices that aren't the best, and when they are not 'perfect'.

We need to let them know over and over again that we do love who they are, just because of who they ARE, not because of what they do (although we may value that and admire it and appreciate it of course).

In the days of pandemic, it is even easier to lose sight of our unconditional love for our partner – we are both under extraordinary, extra stressors. We may be angry at the world; we may be down or depressed or anxious. But this is the time we need to reach out even more to let them know how much we love them just for who they are.

We can say it:

"I love you."

"I love your kind heart, your gentleness, that you're such a loving person."

But it is just as important to show them: a gentle touch, a hug, a squeeze, being playful.

When we show our love in a way that is meaningful to them (see the chapter on love languages) they feel that depth of closeness and connection and interestingly so do we in our expressing it.

That is the paradox of the mutuality of loving. Even if only one expresses it, we both can feel it!

20

Optimists & Pessimists: The crisis is half-full

They say that optimists have a solution for every problem and pessimists have a problem for every solution. This little quip, although grossly oversimplified, does hold a grain of truth.

Optimists and pessimists think in very different ways. The optimist tends to believe that good things are likely to happen and that bad events are isolated and external. Meanwhile, the pessimist thinks that bad things are a common occurrence and that bad events are the likely course of things *ad infinitum*. They also see themselves as part of what is wrong.

Imagine that an optimist and a pessimist each have a dog.

Imagine they take their dogs to the dog park and after a few minutes it runs off and they cannot see them anymore. The optimist's first thoughts will be that their dog is alright, it's just running around, and will return soon – after all, dogs are taken to such parks to run freely.

The pessimists will immediately think the dog has been stolen or hurt and that it's his fault for not watching more carefully.

While they will both look for their dog, their approach to the same situation is night and day.

There is a difference between being positive and naive. There is also a difference between being negative and careful. Understanding that problems can arise does not make one is a pessimist. Nor does having a positive outlook make one out-to-lunch with no sense of reality.

Being in a pandemic is going to bring out very different reactions from optimists and pessimists. If they are in a couple confining together, it can get pretty interesting, not to say challenging. An optimist with a pessimist may feel dragged down. Yet, a pessimist may also raise their partners' hopes and help them to see that things will improve. Or a pessimist may lose patience with the optimist's belief that everything will turn out okay.

By definition, public health crises are bad things. Very bad things. Many people are getting sick and dying, people are losing jobs, the economy is going down. At the time of writing, there is yet no vaccine, times are unpredictable and we don't know when things will get back to normal. As a pessimist, I would think this is the beginning of the end and that there will be a continued downward spiral. Endless news and posts would feed and support this worldview. As an optimist, I would focus on the progress made in research, the ways it can be managed and how the time in lockdown can be used in ways that increase growth and wellbeing.

It's all a matter of perception.

And as such, it is not that one is right or wrong *per se*. It is that one way of thinking is better for health and more productive in terms of taking action, as opposed to blaming oneself and fearing a world of doom and gloom.

But it's a difficult situation. There is no getting around that. There are, however, ways of thinking that are more useful and hopeful, not to mention is associated with increased self-esteem, ability to handle stress, to bounce back from sickness, and is simply better for emotional and psychological wellbeing.

———

Activity

Shut off the news for a week, print, online and social media. The continued onslaught of devastation around the world can make us all feel like pessimists. It's draining and hard to see the silver linings. Sometimes it's a good idea to just walk away from things that get us down.

———

Questions for Reflection

Do I believe things will improve? Why or why not? What does my partner think?

Do I tend to think in a way that is conducive to wellbeing?

What things make me feel optimistic? What makes me feel pessimistic?

Rather than being a pessimist, might I have depression that requires the support of mental health specialists?

21

Speaking the Languages of Love

I cannot say it better than Gary Chapman said it in his book called *"The Five Love Languages"* (Chapman, 2015). So I'm not even going to try.

In summary, the book discusses how each person has a different way (language) of expressing love. I am sure we have seen this in our own families and networks of friends. And this remains true within our own romantic relationships. The five languages are:

- Words of Affirmation
- Quality Time
- Receiving Gifts
- Acts of Service
- Physical Touch

There are great online quizzes and fun resources, a couple of which are mentioned at the end of this chapter.

So instead, let me tell a little story to illustrate this point.

My husband. When we first met (so actually before he was my husband), I was having trouble with work. I felt like my boss didn't understand me and wasn't supportive enough. She would dismiss my issues or expect me to resolve them all by myself. As a result, *she* became my problem.

Most days after work, when I would see my husband for dinner, he had lots of great advice about how I could handle her, what I could have done, what I should have done, but I still could do, what he would do, books I could read, and methodologies I could employ to get my boss to understand my position.

I found his approach very sweet. He wanted to help, he wanted to support me. He was listening to my problems and wanted to see me get through the tough times. He was doing everything right.

And it was driving me up the freaking wall.

But how could I say to him, my new boyfriend, that all his care and concern were driving me crazy?

Just the fact that he was giving me advice became a trigger for me (see the chapter on triggers). The moment he would start saying, "You know, you could..." I could feel my stomach cramping up and my shoulders tightening.

I came to realize - this is his language of love.

I didn't know how to read his behavior at the time because I couldn't remove myself from the situation far enough to understand that from where he stood, he was doing an act of love.

Eventually, I told him that his way of showing his care just wasn't working for me. Granted my pitch was a little elevated, along with my volume, but I was able to explain to him what I needed from him, and perhaps more importantly, what I did not need from him.

I can still remember the look of surprise on his face at how his well-meaning gesture had not had the positive effect he'd intended.

The good news is that both he and I are very physically affectionate as a way of showing our love. So while we may have other ways of demonstrating our care, when it comes to snuggle time, we are always on the same wavelength.

I really recommend you read the book "The Five Love Languages" by Gary Chapman, take some of the quizzes, and most importantly talk about it with your partner. It may be that we also have to adapt how *we* show love so that it better fulfills the needs of our partner.

———

Activity

Do some of the love language quizzes together, ideally in a relaxed environment, without other pressures weighing in.

Compare your results.

Are there any surprises there? In your own mind, how can you use this knowledge to better speak the love language preferred by your partner?

Check out the Five Love Languages website:

- https://www.5lovelanguages.com/
- https://www.5lovelanguages.com/quizzes/

Another "What's your love language?" Quiz:

- https://www.psychologies.co.uk/tests/whats-your-love-language.html

————

Questions for Reflection

How does my partner demonstrate their love for me?

What is their preferred way of receiving love?

How do I currently demonstrate my love for my partner? Do I show my love in a way that my partner would like to receive it? Are there ways that I can be more attentive to their love language?

What have I left unsaid to my partner, in hopes that they would understand what I wanted from them? How can I communicate my wants and needs in a way that is not discouraging or demeaning of their love language while making very clear what I would like from them?

22

Expectations and Reality: A few words

"But if you really loved me, you would know what I want!"

Hmmm... I once really believed those words. In fact, I even said them! Of course, I was very young and newly married. My husband would say: "I DO really love you, but I'm not a mind-reader!" Once I learned to express what it was I wanted and he was (mostly!) responsive to me, I realized that those were fairy-tale expectations that no human being can live up to.

How can we determine if our expectations are far out of line with reality, or even possibility?

Let us first look at discouragement and what that means on a personal level.

One way to determine the level of discouragement in ourselves is to see the difference between our "Self-Ideal" (Expectation) and our "Self-Image" (Reality). The greater the distance between the high expectation and the lower reality, the more discouraged we feel. We may have unachievable expectations, like perfectionism. Any small step short of that is perceived as a failure. Hence, our belief may be that no matter how hard we try we can never meet our expectations and so we are a failure.

Similarly, in today's world of social media, how often do we feel as though others' lives are so great, and ours are somehow less so? How often have I heard in counseling, "Everyone else's life is so fun, great, awesome, happy, and look at me? Why can't I be that way?"

This is another recipe for discouragement.

Or: "They look so happy! Why can't my relationship be like that?"

Again, we perceive a huge gap between what we would *expect* our lives to be (like other people) and where we *perceive* our own lives (as inferior). The self-ideal, the expectation to be like the others - is false. No one has the perfect life as portrayed in social media.

The perceived reality is also false because we are comparing ourselves; all we see is what is negative, and not the actual reality of our lives! The more discouraged we feel, in ourselves, or in our relationship, the harder it is for us to focus the actual reality of the strengths and positives we have right now.

Everything is even more challenging to deal with in lockdown as perceptions become intensified, and not necessarily in a way that makes us happy.

We can apply this more directly to our relationship as well. Often we have unrealistic expectations of our partner. (See the example above where I expected my husband not just to know what I wanted but to do it!) When he didn't read my mind and didn't do what I wanted, I actually did unrealistically feel that he did not love me, which was the furthest from the truth.

I needed to see the Reality that:

1. My belief that "love means you knew everything I need" was false;
2. Doing exactly what I wanted wasn't what unconditional love was about at all.

I had to learn that my Expectations were not achievable in the way I thought they should be and that the Reality was that love involves not mind-reading but the work of communication, commitment, cooperation - and not always getting my way!

Once I understood this, my discouragement in my relationship shifted to that of encouragement because my expectations shifted to reality and not fantasy. I was able to accept his real love in a way that made me feel loved and not bereft because of my own unrealistic expectations.

23

A Lockdown Love Story: Get home quick!

I met Ed in August 2019. In December 2019, he moved in with me. Even though it was kind of quick, for us it was the right decision. I remember telling him that since he traveled all the time and was away during the week, that living together would be relatively easy as it would rarely be him and I alone at the apartment.

And indeed we started settling into a rhythm that worked for us. We both had to adjust. In some ways, I had more adjusting to do, because he had moved into *my* apartment, and I wasn't accustomed to sharing that space.

Then, in February 2020, just a couple of months after we'd moved in together, Ed left for a three-week mission in Saint Pierre, and we didn't foresee any problem with his trip.

It was while he was away that the virus started causing more and more difficulty, and we were starting to see what was coming.

Texting through Whatsapp was how we talked through our plans, even if it had been a giant pain for me to get Whatsapp in the first place.

Ed's trip was the reason I got Whatsapp installed on my phone, and it was a horrible experience. I won't go into the details, but in short, my phone was too old, I had to get a new one, then the sim card didn't work, so hours and hours later I finally had it installed. It was extremely frustrating, but ultimately it was through Whatsapp texts that I realized he was quite anxious about the growing epidemic.

And whether he could get home.

He would have to fly through both Canada and the US before getting home to France, but we could see that things were not going well in any country and especially for air travel this was a real problem.

Then, just like that, everything suddenly locked down in Saint Pierre. Poor Ed was the only one in his hotel with nowhere to go, and we still weren't sure he was going to make it back.

So our lockdown started on different continents.

We were so focused on getting Ed home that we weren't thinking about the idea of being locked down together. Everything in my life was about waiting for Ed to get home.

Then he got on the plane, and just in time!

The next day the borders were closed. All flights canceled.

But he was on his way home. I was so relieved...

...And worried. He had to take five flights through three countries just as this epidemic was starting. So many airports, so many worries.

When he finally got home he was jetlagged, exhausted, and feeling unwell.

Really unwell.

I rushed to the pharmacy to get a thermometer, but can you imagine trying to find a thermometer at the beginning of lockdown for a virus? I had to go to four or five pharmacies before I could even find one.

That was hard. He was sick, we didn't know what it was. It was hard.

So there we were, locked down, Ed was unwell, and in our few months of living together, we hadn't yet experienced sickness, especially with the question of COVID going around.

I had to convince him to go to bed and relax because he felt he had to be up and doing things. And of course, we had to manage the fear of 'What if it's COVID?'

Fortunately, lots of sleep later, he was feeling better.

At first, I had a hard time understanding what "confinement" (as lockdown was called in France) meant. I knew I had to stay at home, but it took me a long time to really *feel* what confinement was. It meant I wouldn't be going to work. I wouldn't be seeing my students for a long time - we didn't even know how long it would be.

I'd thought, "Okay, this will last a few weeks. Then things will go back to normal."

After all, I've never lived through a serious epidemic...

In fact, the first three weeks of lockdown were wonderful!

Ed and I hadn't seen each other for a long time, so the time together was great. We were both working... from home. In a very small space. One small bedroom, one open office space, and a bathroom. And we both had to use video and speak in this little space. But we were figuring it out.

The people we were talking to could always hear the other person. Even the neighbor's dog would interrupt us by barking. I'd have to ask Ed to speak lower or remember that I was there. We were just so busy that we hardly noticed that the end of the day had come, and we would take our 'one-hour government-permitted exercise' and go for a walk together. It was lovely and it became our routine.

We walked through the neighborhood. We walked up the big hill to the church, we walked along the sea and in front of the beach. That hour was our time to walk and talk.

That one hour out together - I just loved it.

It signaled the end of our workday and that we were back together as a couple, even though we'd spent the whole day in the same little space. It was the moment when Ed could finally let go of his workday we could be closer together.

Yes, the first three weeks were great. He started making home-made bread knowing that I love bread and I couldn't get it myself anymore. That was so sweet.

But then the lockdown continued.

Many things changed and it got harder for us.

My classes had ended, so I essentially became confined to the bedroom while Ed worked in the other part of the apartment. I don't like my bedroom for anything except sleeping.

Then we lost our routine.

That made it harder for Ed to switch off, especially since his work was trying to adapt to the situation by having him take on different activities. All that meant Ed's stress level rose.

Things in my job were up in the air too; some of my students had fallen ill and we couldn't see where things were going.

I was spending so much time on my own and our evening walks just didn't happen anymore.

Tension between us increased.

I tried all kinds of things. Exercising more, reading, thinking...

But he was stuck in his world and I was growing resentful.

I realized that I had to acknowledge my own feelings. I was worried about work and my own mental state, and I was seeing new sides to him and I didn't know how to help him.

We sat down and talked about what was happening. We can talk about anything - just not always on the spot. That's one of the reasons I've believed this relationship can work.

I broached the subject by starting with me. How I wasn't feeling well, I knew I was being less patient. And how he was in his own state, which was ultimately affecting me too. But I wasn't sure if I was explaining it in a way that he could hear.

At last, I said, "I don't want us to live this way. I can't live this way." I explained that we needed a different dynamic between us because I wanted to be with him and needed him to be more present.

Here's the greatest thing about having Ed as a partner: he is willing to do what it takes to make things work. He really wants me to be happy and he takes concrete steps to make it happen.

And we did it! We found a way to get through that challenging time. This is what we did:

1. First, we diagnosed why it had gotten harder, what had changed in our way of life together.

2. Then we re-started the things that had gone well - we started our walks again. Having simple conversations in the evening together about things that weren't about work. In fact, we made a point of not talking about work at all!

3. I took better care of my own needs. If I needed to go for a walk, I just did it. I didn't wait for him anymore because it wasn't always what he wanted to do.

4. We found some nice moments together. Having a beer, sharing memories, talking about friends.

5. We began looking ahead - projects, ideas, future trips when we could travel again. How we would revise the plans we'd previously had. Fortunately, we both like doing things near home (even in our own neighborhood) so we're very compatible this way, which made planning easier. While we were disappointed about having to change big travel plans, especially for me to meet his parents, we found another solution. We focused instead on what we could do.

6. We're considering new living arrangements with more physical space, personal space, and mental space. Because we live in *my* flat, we are thinking through ways that my flat could be *our* flat. But we're also thinking about getting a new place with

more space so we don't fall over each other in the kitchen anymore!

Overall, we're being more communicative about how to improve things. We talk about words that are triggers and speak up when we need certain routines kept in place. We're both getting more sensitive to the other's needs.

I am thankful that Ed is so willing to listen; he makes such great efforts. He really tries to adjust, even at the small things. He makes me laugh so much. The trick for us these days is for him to be able to relax with me, and for me to work on being more patient with him. Patience is hard for me. That's when I start feeling my age and the weight of the past on me. It's harder for me to adapt. I have my habits, and I like my habits.

But when he makes me laugh, everything else gets undone and I see all the things in him that I love.

Now that we've come through this lockdown, we know we are together because we choose to be, not because we're dependent on each other. The lockdown helped us to recognize that. And for me, that's a good place to start the next phase of our relationship.

24

Equality and Mutual Respect

Equality. Love requires a partnership of equals. But all too often we mistake equality for sameness – we're both just as good at running the house, at bringing in an income, at aerobics.

This is where our thinking is wrong.

Equality has nothing to do with being the same, doing the same things, or even being equally good, or bad, at different tasks. What equality does mean is equal WORTH – equal value as human beings with equal right to dignity and respect.

In terms of intimacy, this means that we treat the other person with respect and believe them to be as worthy of respect as we are. If each believes the other to be equal, there need never be a test to see who is better, or who is on top, or who is the boss.

The energy wasted on those kinds of futile and destructive issues can be spent in joining with our intimate other in cooperation. Here lies the real power over our lives, in joining our forces together to create a third entity beyond 'You' and 'Me'. That third entity is 'Us'.

In the 'us,' we can turn our intimate relationships into a place where we sense and act on our own worth, strengths, and personal power combined with the worth, strengths, and power of the other most important person in our lives.

What we hope to share in our love partnership is 'mutual respect' – where each of us respects ourselves and our beloved partner. This term is used in teaching children to respect themselves and their caregivers, but it applies equally to a loving partnership. "Mutual respect based on the assumption of equality is the inalienable right of all human beings." (Dreikurs, Rudolf and Margaret Goldman 1986).

Mutual respect means loving and accepting ourselves and our partner for who we are, as we are (see the chapter on Unconditional Positive Regard). It does not mean not working on our issues, but that in spite of our faults, and failings, and imperfections, we still accept and love and respect the other for who they are. It is one of the most profound foundations of an abiding love relationship.

Mutual respect is a must, but showing it and feeling and believing in respect for each other can really only be effective when we show, feel, and believe in respect for ourselves.

(After all, if you are my equal and I don't think very highly of myself then you can't be much either.) Self-respect is a critical part of mutual respect.

One of the beauties of intimate love is that often the one we love mirrors us in a way we haven't recognized before.

So mutual and self-respect can often blossom simultaneously.

This does not mean that we change or become something other than what we already are. But we finally recognize, through the eyes of the beloved other, our value and worth, and we can finally function and love in the nurturing atmosphere of equality and respect (Nisan 1990).

25

Active Listening: Hearing and being heard

How often have we felt that our partner, our friend, our co-worker, or anyone really, isn't listening to what we are saying, let alone, understanding it? It can cause a lot of friction, arguments, misunderstandings, upsets, tears, and frustration, especially in our most intimate relationships.

There are a number of ways to let our partner know we are listening to them, with our attention, not just with our ears, and this chapter deals with the first very simple step in what can be called active listening (Rogers 2015).

Sometimes we talk to our partner while they are working on the computer, or watching TV or the birds, or reading a book, or even just sitting next to us, and we get no response. Sometimes we don't get any acknowledgment that they even know we are talking! If you have ever experienced this, you know how frustrating it can be.

In order to not get upset or frustrated, the first step is to make sure you actually have their attention.

It took me a long time to realize that even though I walked into the room where my husband was, and started talking, even about something I thought was interesting, he didn't even notice I was there! At first, I got frustrated. After all, if he walked into the room and started talking to me, I would notice and either stop what I was doing and listen or, at the very least, I would acknowledge his presence!

But once I figured out he truly was absorbed in what he was doing, and that he was not intentionally slighting me or ignoring me, I was able to solve that problem pretty efficiently. I would either make sure first that I had his attention, but I would also ensure that this was a good time to talk, and if not, when. This really helped with my ability to communicate in a much calmer manner.

There is another important side to communication though, and that is, how do we actually show our partner that we are listening when they are talking to us?

It's much simpler than people realize, and here are the ways in a nutshell:

1. Eye contact: look at them when they are talking to you. Don't gaze off into the sky, or the garden, or your phone!
2. Nod your head: if they are saying something you agree with, at the very least, just nod your head to show that you are taking it in and agreeing.
3. Don't interrupt: I was so guilty of this, that I know my husband was hugely frustrated with me over it. When we interrupt it means we are more in our own thoughts and not really letting our partner finish theirs.

4. Other body language: Lean in, touch their arm, anything to show you are present and listening.
5. Simple verbal cues like: 'mmhmm', or 'yes', or 'ohhh'. Just some small sign that you are present. An alternative to just head nodding!

There have been times when I have talked to people, or rather they have talked to me, and I have used these simple techniques. The feedback I got was after even barely saying a word was,

---

"Wow, you are a good listener!"

The following two chapters on reflecting words and listening with your heart talk about the next levels of communication, which we need in our intimate relationships to help keep the conversations and closeness going. We need this throughout our relationship and especially in the intense times of lockdown.

———

Activity

There are many practice exercises on active listening: search Active Listening Exercises online.

26

How to Feel Heard: Reflecting your partner's words

The next steps in Active Listening are:

1. letting your partner know you hear what they are saying, and
2. letting your partner know that you have heard them.

The best way to describe this stage of listening is to look at an exercise demonstrating how it is done. Then you and your partner can practice together in order to get in the habit of more effective communication.

Steps:

1. Sit across from each other. Partner A briefly speaks about a topic, usually of some importance or value to him or her, but not a 'hot potato' topic. ('Hot Potato' Topics are those points of contention or disagreement between the two of you that are very difficult to resolve, and are currently unresolved. See the chapter on 'Hot Potato Topics').

2. Partner B listens, without interruption. (Simple, usually!)

3. When Partner A has finished, then Partner B repeats back what he heard her say, as closely as possible.

4. Now Partner A must listen closely to what Partner B is saying until they are done

5. Partner A then either says, "Yes, you got it! I do feel that you understood what I was saying," or "Not quite, you got most or some of it, except for ..."

6. Here's the trick again: Partner B must really listen to this revision, and then you can guess the next step...

7. Partner B repeats back again what they thought they heard. It is okay to use some of the same words even, just not all of them.

8. Partner A listens and says, "Yes, you got it," or "Almost...", and then repeats if there is still something missing. This goes on until Partner A really feels B got it, which is when they say,

"You got it. You heard me!"

9. SWITCH!!

It can actually be a fun exercise if each of you takes it that way. This is meant to be a way to improve your communication in a lockdown, since we all know that right now communication can get even more muddled than usual.

Here's an example:

A: I had such a good time talking to your parents on Zoom yesterday. The only thing was your mother again mentioned the time that I forgot her birthday. I know she was kind of joking, but I felt bad back then, and I have tried to make it up to her, but it just brought back all those old feelings for me again.

B: You enjoyed talking to my parents yesterday. The only problem was mom reminded you of that time you forgot her birthday and you felt bad again.

A: Almost: I have really tried since then to make it up to her, and give her really nice gifts on her birthday, but when she mentioned it again, kind of joking, I felt bad all over again.

B: So, you have really tried hard since the time you did forget her birthday, to be extra nice, with special gifts and everything, but when she said it again yesterday, even in fun, you felt the old bad feelings.

A: You got it! I really feel like you heard what I was saying.

Hopefully, that little example gives you an idea of how it can go. Over time and with practice, this kind of listening and acknowledgment of being heard can actually become incorporated into your way of communicating as a couple.

But we're not done yet! There is one more even deeper level of communication that will be described in the chapter on Listening with Your Heart.

———

Activity

There are many practice exercises on reflective listening. Search online for Reflective Listening Exercises.

27

Listening with your Heart:
Reflection of feelings

This next section talks about how to know in your heart that you are not just heard, but that you are deeply understood. It also covers how we communicate that back to our partner in a way that is deep and effective.

When we are in an intimate relationship with someone, it means that we want to connect at the most profound level with that person. Understanding how they feel and showing them that we understand are ways we can deepen our connection.

Again, this is best exemplified by the same exercise in the previous chapter, but this time we are not just repeating *what* the person said but also the *feelings* they expressed, implicitly or explicitly.

Let's use the same example from the last chapter and add this more emotionally connecting element.

A: I had such a good time talking on Zoom to your parents yesterday. The only thing was your mother mentioned the time that I forgot her birthday. I know she was kind of joking, but I felt bad then, and I have tried to make it up to her, but it just brought back all those old feelings again.

B: You enjoyed talking to Mom and Dad yesterday. Mom talked again about how you forgot her birthday that one time, and it reminded you of how bad you felt when you did that.

A: Yes, you have the first part of it. When she reminded me of it yesterday it made me feel badly all over again, even though I have tried so hard to make up for it since then.

B: It sounds like when she brought it up again yesterday, even though she was doing it as a joke, you felt those first really bad feelings you had when it happened.

A: Yes. But there's more I think. I've tried so hard to make it up but I wonder if it will ever be enough.

B: Oh, so I wonder if it could be that what you may be feeling is discouraged that you'll never be able to do enough to make it up to her.

A: You're right! I do feel very discouraged. You get me.

So perhaps you can see how with teasing out bit by bit, Partner B actually in a way helped Partner A figure out the deeper feelings that they may not have exactly expressed.

It is communication at a very in-depth level and perhaps you can even see how this discussion may have even brought them closer, and opening up a conversation on how to deal with this issue.

This is a way we can come even closer to empathy with our partner, which is one of the fundamentals of a close and intimate relationship.

There is no perfect way to do this. It just takes cooperation, sometimes a sense of humor. It also takes a sincere desire to work on our communication with one another, ultimately with the goal of connecting even more deeply.

————

Activity

As mentioned in the previous chapter, there are many practice exercises on reflective listening. For reflection of feelings, search online for "listening with reflection of feelings".

PART IV

HOW CAN I DO BETTER FOR US? SELF-AWARENESS FOR A JOYFUL COUPLE THROUGH ALL OF THIS

Master the Pre-Apology, aka the Wake-Up Funk

Inevitably, there are going to be days when you wake up and the world just sucks.

Perhaps you'll be able to recognize right away why you feel this way. Maybe the dog two floors below was howling at the midnight moon. Maybe your partner was stealing the covers (again). Maybe your nose is stuffed because of the darn nature outside and so you could hardly get a wink of sleep and instead woke up choking on your own phlegm.

In these situations, it is easy to see why you feel like crap.

But some days it won't be so easy.

You'll wake up after having slept normally, with your alarm at just the right hour, coffee already brewing in the kitchen.

And you'll feel it. The wake-up funk.

While the wake-up funk can affect us during regular periods of our lives, it is especially acute and destructive during a global pandemic. In regular times, you leave the house, you change your surroundings and hopefully your state of mind with it.

The wake-up funk can be disastrous in a relationship, specifically because it stimulates confrontation based on very little input. In other words, you will be triggered, and even though the trigger may be a real thing, your reaction will be disproportionately out of sync with that trigger.

Enter: The Pre-Apology

The Pre-Apology goes something like this:

"Sweetie, I woke up in a funk."

"Oh geez, again?"

Resist! This alone will feel like a cause for explosion. Resist the urge to react! Instead, consider the following:

"I can't put my finger on it, but I'm just not feeling right. Something, and maybe something really small, is going to put me over the edge today. So I want to apologize in advance in case I explode on you. Which by the way, is more likely if you say things like 'Oh geez, again?' So maybe consider thinking those words rather than saying them out loud next time. In any case, I'm sorry if my wake-up funk gets taken out on you."

Some people can't stand apologizing. They resist with extra fervor the idea of the pre-apology. Their arguments include the following:

- My feelings are real feelings. I shouldn't have to apologize for them.

- She does things that genuinely piss me off. Sometimes I think she does them on purpose.

- He doesn't care about my apology; he doesn't want me to explode, ever.

- Apologies are for wusses.

If one of these arguments, or another of the similar ilk, come to mind for you as you're reading this chapter, I really encourage you to re-think. An apology is a signal that you are considering your partner. A Pre-Apology is a signal that you recognize your own personal limitations.

Lockdown is particularly effective at highlighting our personal limitations in a relationship. This means that apologizing - real apologizing, meaningful apologizing - is not just about the act itself.

Pre-Apologizing is an act of recognition.

For it to be effective, it cannot be done with the purpose of eliciting a certain response from your partner, but rather it is a way of communicating with them. The Pre-Apology is a signal. What your partner does with that signal is up to them. But if during the day, that funk sneaks in and sets you off, you can reference the pre-apology as a way to help your partner understand why it is happening.

For people with generally even-keel personalities, this is an especially effective tool during lockdown. That's because there will be moments when you act out of character, and your partner may not recognize the behavior in you at all. This can be very destabilizing in a relationship. Naming the wake-up funk, calling it out, and apologizing for it, lets you use it to build your relationship in this not-normal time.

————

Activity

The next time you open your eyes and realize you are in a wake-up funk, try to notice the signals you have in your own body. Is your breathing different? Do you have a sensation of weight on your chest? Do you want to bury yourself under the pillow when normally you hop out of bed? Do the chirping birds you normally love suddenly grate on your nerves? The wake-up funk physically expresses itself differently for everyone. You cannot practice the pre-apology if you cannot recognize what the wake-up funk feels like.

————

Questions for Reflection

How do I normally feel when I wake up?

What physical sensations do I have that indicate I'm in a wake-up funk?

Am I willing to pre-apologize? If not, why not? What beliefs do I have that might prevent me from being able to signal to my partner my current mental state?

Do I have any deep-set beliefs about apologizing that might be interfering with the quality of my relationship?

29

Finding and Keeping Your Happy

Ten things you didn't know about black holes.
Can anything move faster than the speed of light?
Do we really need a theory of everything?

She stares at you, stoic, and explains these difficult concepts with such clarity, it is like she's showing you how the blender works. Except it's about the known and unknown universe. This is Sabine Hossenfelder on her YouTube channel called *Science without the gobbledygook.*

Then there is Sabine Hossenfelder the singer. Yes, the singer. There is another channel for that. In her song Ivory Tower, with lights sparkling in the background, she sings,

There is an office, at the end of the corridor.
You all know, whose it is.
It's professor Dr. famous you've been coming for.
To shake his hand and smell his breath.
But the professor has no time.
He has got a paper to write.

*And the next thing on his list is to prove the universe does not
    exist.*
We have no place for cowards in the halls of the Ivory Tower.
How can they fail to see that the next big thing is me?

I love her.

I love her because she is doing her thing without abandon. You
get the sense that she doesn't really care what the world thinks;
this is something she would do in any case, and it just so
happens we have a window into her life.

And so it is with me and dancing. I dance when I'm happy. I
dance when I'm not. I dance because it's Tuesday afternoon. I
dance even after my husband, concerned about the architec-
tural integrity of our century-old building, tells me the apartment is shaking and the neighbors will complain and maybe I
will fall right through the floor. I half-listen, smiling a little and
I dance some more. I can't help it.

Dancing is my happy. It is my happy place and my happy time.
I always feel good doing it. And I did it every single day of the
four months of lockdown. I sometimes wondered, will the
downstairs neighbor catch me if I pirouette right through into
her living room?

As for my partner, he prefers to build civilizations. He speaks
with bearded kings and haughty queens adorned in jewels and
scowls. I see his world and his forests and planes circling over
verdant lands from a distance. He asks me if it should be a
socialist regime. Not this time honey, I say. Playing video games
is his happy. For me (except for interactive or dance ones), it is
really not my thing.

And it doesn't have to be. We let each other be free and find and keep our own happy. We might murmur a little now and then, but it's understood. I know that building worlds calms him down and makes him happy. He knows that getting my dance on is my therapy, my happy, my safe space.

That's why I dig Sabine. She's doing her happy. And I would encourage everyone one of you to find your happy and do it too. As much as you possibly can.

———

Activity

Reflect on what makes you feel wonderful, happy, and where hours pass as if in an instant. When are you the happiest? It might take some reflection and journaling. Looking back to what you did as a child that was freeing. Is it writing, art, singing, dancing, playing games, puzzles, excising, or reading? Or something else entirely?

Then do it.

Also, as much as you enjoy your free happy time, be fine with how your partner expresses their happy. You don't have to like it and you don't have to participate. Just let them be.

———

Questions for Reflection

When do I feel most happy?

What do I love to do?

How can I incorporate that into my daily routine?

30

Quality Time Together

An old adage, to spend quality time together.

When you hear 'quality time', what do you think of? Maybe snuggling up by the fireplace? Or going out for a fancy dinner? Perhaps playing a good game of badminton.

You probably didn't think of being trapped in a one-bedroom apartment for weeks on end.

Even when lockdown lifts, traces of the time we have spent in close captivity with our partners inevitably have an impact on how we perceive each other.

Both during lockdown and after lockdown, the idea of "quality time" can seem irrelevant, redundant, or borderline ridiculous.

But let's scratch those judgments, and start fresh.

Time does not equal quality time.

I'm stating the obvious, I know. The issue for me during lockdown and thereafter was not whether the idea of quality time remained important, it was how to have quality time when I was so sick of looking at my husband's face. I love him and I love his face, I just didn't want to look at it anymore.

There are many activities throughout this book that can be defined as 'spending quality time'. So this chapter is focused a little bit more on mindset than the activity of having quality time itself.

Were you like me, feeling like time during lockdown had gone into some deep black hole, disappeared, never to return? Looking in the mirror to find a new grey hair, a new wrinkle, or a general malaise with life when usually I'm a happy-go-lucky, grateful, and positive person?

Time during lockdown for me was both an enemy and a savior. A savior, because where I live, we had no other way of managing the virus' spread. Living in France during the outbreak meant that there was an early onset of drastic cases and a heavy caseload in general. As someone with a pre-existing condition, the risks were that much greater.

And I really like living. I intend to do it for as long as possible. I don't need to take any risks.

So in my head, I was able to approach the period of lockdown from a very rational perspective, watching the pandemic's figures as they grew and then diminished and then grew again...

A funny side-story.

The day before lockdown hit, I went to work from a café around the corner. It was my habitual café across from the Mediterranean Sea, where they still only charge €1.60 for an espresso. By the way, getting used to drinking espressos took me quite a long time, but now I'll never go back.

While there, I took off my Fitbit. As someone who works from home, I bought a Fitbit long before it was trendy to help me make sure I got up from my desk from time to time. But when I'm working on my computer, it always gets in the way, so I take it off. And on that day, March 16th, 2020, I left it at the café on the table. Normally that would be no big deal as I know the people who work there, except that the following day, we went into total lockdown and all cafés were closed and my Fitbit was held hostage.

Fast forward a number of months, when things had opened up again, cafés being one of the later businesses allowed to open, I went back to my favorite café, not expecting anything, because why would a Fitbit still be there all these months later?

I asked the owner if there was any chance she had seen a little black watch left behind the day before lockdown, and sure enough, there was.

When I got home, still pleasantly surprised that I had it at all, I plugged it in and the date that appeared was March 24th.

By that time, it was June 23rd.

That summed up exactly how I felt about time.

Three months of my life had dissipated into thin air.

But, of course, that wasn't true. I had been living with my husband all of that time. I had written a book (not this one). We had some family crises together where we have been concerned for members of our family who had fallen ill. Much had been lived during those three months, and yet there was a big part of me that when it said March 24th on the watch, it wanted to believe that indeed we were still back then.

Back to spending quality time together. As I mentioned most of this book is dedicated to different ways of spending quality time together, so I refer you to those other chapters for tips and tricks on this subject.

However, this is my golden nugget of realization during that three months' vacuum:

In order to spend quality time together, we must spend quality time apart.

And now I suggest you go to the next chapter, aptly named "Spending Time Apart".

———

Questions for Reflection:

There's just one.

Have I made a special effort to spend sufficient real quality time with my partner?

Quality Time Apart: Creating
space

Spending quality time apart. Hmmm.

Quality time together is the easier part, because so much of this book is specifically about that.

This chapter is harder.

Quality time apart.

The first challenge comes during the period of lockdown. How can we possibly have quality time apart when living within the same quarters ALL THE TIME? Of course, this is even harder if you're in a studio, one-bedroom, or apartment without any outside space.

And the fact is that even once lockdown lifts, we still live together. We have to spend time together within those four walls, because that's where we live. The aroma of lockdown might still be in the air for weeks and months to come, so how can we not feel confined while still living in the same place where we *were* confined?

Separation is physical and mental.

I want to be clear, time apart, as referenced in this chapter, is not about reassessing your relationship. Quite the contrary, it is about being with yourself, while, depending on your own circumstances, being with other people.

Spending quality time apart in order to appreciate your quality time together is the goal here.

Unhealthy habits and ways of relating to each other may have grown between you during lockdown.

Below are some tips and tricks to create healthy habits on each level of what could be called personal space. Some of them get pretty creative, and we encourage you to be as creative as possible.

Creativity, mixing it up, helps keep things fresh. But again, the goal here is not to separate yourself from your partner, but rather to have rich time away from them which you can then bring back into the space when you are together.

PHYSICAL SPACE

A partition:

When we used to take long car trips from Canada to Florida, my brother and I, three years between us, would fight and annoy each other over the course of the 24-hour drive.

So our parents partitioned us.

At first, it was a suitcase propped up in the middle of the back seat, but we found ways of wiggling her fingers around it, just enough space to poke at the other's shoulder or ear.

So then our parents created a custom wall out of cardboard. I have no idea where they found a box that big. It filled the space between us.

Fortunately, my brother and I get along much better now (especially since he lives in Canada and I live in France - just kidding - love you, bro).

The idea here is to have a physical thing that provides a visual divide for some privacy.

Safe other spaces:

Do you have a friend who goes out during the day whose apartment or home you could use while they are there and you and your partner are both teleworking?

The glorious outdoors:

While trying to work with a laptop from a park bench introduces new challenges, some good quality headphones or even earplugs may provide you with enough focus to work for a public space, out in the open, but away from home where your partner is.

Allocated hours:

A friend of mine lives in a normal-sized apartment for Europe, quite small on North American standards. Both she and her partner were working from home with no separate space available other than the bedroom. They designated times of day when each of them would work in the open space or the bedroom. The routine helped them to focus, and to be in the same space, while feeling like they had specific times when they were scheduled apart (though in close confinement).

Post-lockdown space:

There's this funny phenomenon that seems to be underway post-lockdown in many parts of the world. Couples are struggling to rediscover their footing in what we would think would be relatively "normal times" again. And yet so much remains abnormal.

Couples come out of lockdowns different than they went in.

It may be that some dependence has grown between partners. Conversely, you might also be dying to get away and into the free air.

My husband is a very noisy man, between opera singing lessons on Zoom, playing the balalaika (a Russian string instrument), and general chit chat at the dog. Personally, all I'd been craving is quiet. It wasn't easy to find in a busy city in France.

Others may be itching for more activity and liveliness after so many days quiet at home.

Navigating all this isn't easy for any of us. Some couples may have adapted well, while others struggled under any one of the many stresses.

Creating some physical space, even after lockdown, remains important for a healthy functioning relationship, just as it was before lockdown.

As mentioned at the beginning of this book, your couple might need some professional advice on ways to manage these various stressors after lockdown ends. This is not a period for shame or fear of professional help. Please do not hesitate to seek out support from a professional, either for yourself or as a couple, if it is going to bring you into a better place together.

This is especially true if anger, frustration, or other heavy feelings have snuck in during this time of uncertainty.

MENTAL SPACE

Phone a Friend:

There was a British game show where if you didn't know the answer, you could 'phone a friend'. What we've learned during the initial months of this outbreak, is that none of us really have the answer. One way to widen the walls of our confined space, whether we be confined according to government decree, confined for our own health, or confined simply by definition of sleeping every night in the same place, phoning a friend takes us out of our immediate space and into a situation that is both social and 'out there'.

I've heard many stories of people reconnecting with lost acquaintances, old friends, and distant family. When the walls of home are closing in, reaching out becomes even more important.

A new hobby for you alone:

At the beginning of this global pandemic, lots of people were espousing the virtues of learning a new skill while in lockdown. That's not what I am suggesting here. That is way too much pressure during a time when there is already significant pressure on us. No, don't write that book you've always wanted to write. No, don't learn Portuguese. No, don't renovate the basement.

Of course, do any of those things if you would really like to. I'm just suggesting that adding any additional pressure that isn't necessary may not serve you well.

What I am suggesting here is a mini hobby. Dabble in something that is yours alone. The more micro you can make it, the better. This will let you have little waves of success and a sense of accomplishment on a rolling basis.

At its smallest, this could be drawing a perfectly symmetrical star.

Moving up a level, maybe you try out that glass etching tool you got under Christmas three years ago. If it fails, great! Now you know and you can give that thing away rather than in taking up space in the closet.

Haiku poetry.

Memorizing Irish ditties (or drinking songs, as you like).

Macramé.

Specific domestic habits:

Another way of delineating some territory (and to stop thinking of all the things your partner should have done around the house) is to volunteer to take on certain domestic activities every day.

It might be as simple as emptying the dishwasher, taking the dog on its morning walk, or making the post-lunch coffee.

Whatever it may be, own it.

There's no getting around the fact that domestic duties become more visible when confined. I was amazed at how many forks we managed to use in a day and in turn all the fork washing that was required.

Turning these duties into personal habits can reduce some of the stress associated with feeling like there's always so much to do around the place.

Earplugs and quiet time:

I cannot stop declaring the unexpected and expected benefits of earplugs. Whether working from home, trying to have some evening quiet, or simply in need of shutting out the rest of the world for a little while, earplugs must be one of the least expensive and nonpermanent ways of changing your environment.

Depending on your circumstances, quiet time with earplugs in, eyes closed or open depending on your preference, reduces stimuli, and can have a very calming effect on the entire neurological system.

Lying on your back, with earplugs in, and conducting a body scan can calm nerves and stimulate new neural activity.

There are many body scan recordings if you would prefer to be guided. They can be found on YouTube, podcasts, and albums for sale. They range from three minutes to twenty-five minutes to an hour. Give it a Google to see the many known benefits from conducting a body scan this way (and use the earplugs to block out any possible interruptions, as they can really destroy the mood).

Challenge a different part of your brain:

Are you usually a very cerebral person, interested in facts, information, history, or hard skills? Try doodling. Or writing a poem. Or finger-painting. Or mad libs. If you normally are living solidly in the present, try going back in time through a documentary or forward in time by reading some articles by 'futurists' and coming up with your own theories.

Are you a creative type, usually spending your time in imaginary worlds, creating art, or engaging socially? Try learning about an ancient society. Or how to fix that leaky faucet yourself. Or how to grow your own vegetables from a balcony flower pot (which may be a very useful skill indeed). Or if you have no green thumb, perhaps a week's worth of recipes from around the world.

There are so many options to choose from and you can even have fun in the choosing.

32

A Lockdown Love Story: Portraits

My partner and I are both journalists who have lived in many parts of the world, including London and Afghanistan. However, it was not until the lockdown that we became colleagues in the same house, despite being together for 25 years. It was interesting to discover the day to day professional routine of my partner in real-time as it's something that we hadn't fully shared before.

I am used to working from home so it was not such a big change for me. In fact, it is something I enjoy. As an editor for many years, I have been doing my own writing and working alongside for years. During the lockdown, I decided to pursue my dream full steam ahead. I have decided to stop working and concentrate finally and fully on that.

I think that communication is key for couples in lockdown. We share a lot and we laugh a lot. We had a lot of fun. One afternoon, we decided to do the Getty Museum challenge where people dress up as portraits. It was great fun to look around the house for various household items and disguise ourselves.

There are endless stories and we still enjoy each other very much. One thing that will be clear in a lockdown is if you even like your partner anymore. You will also know if they like you back. It will become crystal clear. You may love them, but you might not like them much anymore.

Or you may discover that after many years, they still make your heart skip a beat and that butterflies flutter in your stomach. That you still have fun with them. And that after all this time, you two can have a glass of wine, dressed up as works of art, and laugh at the absurdity of it all.

33

All That Which Must Be Accepted

Rather than espousing all the philosophical benefits of acceptance, I'm just going to get real for a minute here.

What's happening in our world does not feel acceptable. Let's take only the global pandemic for a moment.

It doesn't seem right that people are dying from something we know so little about.

It doesn't seem right that people are losing their jobs.

It's particularly unfair for certain populations of people around the world who seem to struggle at every turn.

It's unacceptable that our leaders allow politics to interfere with managing the crisis.

There is a whole lot of stuff in this global pandemic that is not right, not fair, plain unacceptable.

But this is a book about our relationships. Whether in a global pandemic or not, we have to find ways of navigating new challenges together. So let me leave behind all that which is unacceptable and over which we have little control, and bring it back into the realm of our relationships where there is much more we can influence.

Certainly, the global pandemic has been the tipping point for many relationships, and for some couples it is perhaps the most significant obstacle they have faced to date.

The global pandemic is not the only crisis couples have faced. Long before COVID-19, there were tragedies big and small, daily injustices, and macro-level emergencies. So let's bring this down to some of its smallest parts.

How do you eat an elephant? One bite at a time.

What is our first bite of this elephant?

Probably accepting that there will be times when we accept nothing.

And next?

There are lots of places for us to go from here.

Okay, okay. I said I wasn't going to get into the philosophy of acceptance, but bear with me for just a moment here.

A simple list of the physical consequences of not accepting (in bite-size chunks) the situation facing us:

- headaches
- stomach pains
- stomach acid
- fatigue
- cramping
- lack of sleep

A Note on Sleep

Lack of acceptance, fighting against every small thing, can have a direct impact on our ability to fall asleep, stay asleep, and have quality sleep. As anyone who suffers from sleep problems will tell you, it affects all aspects of our well-being. Physical exhaustion, getting injured more easily, diminished mental acumen, ability to concentrate, emotional balance. Small things blow out of proportion. Big things completely overwhelm.

Acceptance matters because fighting against the tide has a cost. Let me be clear, there are certainly times when fighting is important, essential even. When there is systemic injustice, when the weak or vulnerable are being exploited, we must act. I am not suggesting otherwise.

What I am suggesting is that we save the fight for the good fight. The real fights, the hard fights.

And for everything else, we accept.

Let me dive into the details as this philosophizing makes it sound like I am only talking about great big grave issues. I'm not.

I am talking about the very small things. Because the small things start as a scratch, and then they infect.

This is even true in the context of our relationship during a global pandemic, don't you think?

Let's start with ourselves, as this is where we always have the greatest control.

Your list will be different from the one below, which is my list, and it's just a subsection of my larger list of all I had to accept. To treat the small scratches before they became an infected mess.

- I accept that my house will never be as clean as I wanted to be because living in it 100% of the time changes the way it's used. Even after lockdown, certain habits are hard to put back in place. They don't feel natural anymore. Because who wants to be spending time, which could be free time out in the free air, tidying up or doing laundry?

- I accept that my day job is harder than it used to be, and I don't have all the answers anymore.

- I accept that it's a beautiful day, and I can't go to the beach. Instead, I will try to appreciate that the beautiful day exists and the many times I benefited from sunshine and fresh air without knowing how precious it was.

- I accept that I can't travel to see my family right now even though my mother had a big birthday, my brother got engaged, several friends have been diagnosed with cancer and I simply miss home.

Accepting in our couple is a different matter. It requires a certain generosity of spirit that can be hard to come by at some moments. Every relationship is different; the aspects that we had come to rely upon in our partner may not be present during this time.

Or maybe never again.

Here's a list I've heard from couples about what they had to accept:

- I don't know him as well as I thought I did

- My partner is so lazy! How did I not see this before?

- My partner was surprised to see the rhythm of how I work since we've both been working from home. She expected me to be present for lunch. But I sequester myself away for the entire workday in order to keep my focus. She really had to adjust her expectations, because I couldn't work any other way.

- There were times when I was sure he could tell I was suffering, and he did nothing. I had to accept he didn't know what to do when he saw me this way because he had never seen me this way before. And ultimately, I didn't know what to even ask for from him.

- My partner never used to have a temper. Now she does. Where did this come from? If I keep letting myself be pulled into a fight every time she explodes about something insignificant, then our life together is really going to be unpleasant. I had always thought she was the level-headed one.

- I'm working like a fool while my partner tries to find a new job. I know he's doing everything he can, and ultimately he just has more free time than I do right now. But sometimes I just feel so infuriated that I have to work so hard he doesn't. But he is stressed out, and I don't like to see that either.

––––––––

Activity

This isn't everyone's style, but isn't this global pandemic about trying new things?

Sit and close your eyes. Meditate on the things over which you have no control.

Now focus on the small things. Those things, which ultimately are not life and death. Picture them individually.

Laser your focus on one specific thing that has brought you a disproportionate amount of struggle and suffering. Household chores? Volume of the TV? Insensitive comments muttered under your partner's breath?

Now watch it float up into the air, letting it go. Know it will return, but when it does it will not have power over you anymore. Watch it go, a balloon floating up and away, a care or a worry that will not weigh on you in the same way again.

Next time that thing comes back (because these things always come back), remember the balloon. Hold onto the string of it for a moment, if you must, but as soon as possible - let it go.

34

Respect: Again, to see

Etymology. From Middle English **respect**, from Old French **respect**, also respit ("**respect**, regard, consideration"), from Latin respectus ("a looking at, regard, **respect**"), perfect passive participle of respiciō ("look at, look back upon, **respect**"), from re- ("back") + speciō ("to see").

Re: Again
Spect: to see
Respect: Again, to see.

To respect something is to see it, *really* see it, again, as if for the first time. That is, to acknowledge it and its complexities fully. Respect is not shallow. It is not ephemeral. It is deep and it is authentic.

What does respect look like, feel like, sound like? Perhaps it sounds like silence as you turn your phone off to be fully present during dinner. It could feel like a hug when you have both had a hard day. Or silence when you are the early riser and they have yet to meet the day. It may look like concern and encouragement. It feels like you are basking in the sunlight of attention because you are considered and found whole and worthy.

This is respect. This is to look again.

But can we really respect our partner when we do not respect ourselves?

Yes and no.

We can respect others while having little regard for ourselves. I don't believe it is a precursor. But it makes things complicated. Can a person without self-respect bloom under the loving gaze of another who shows them their worth? It can happen. Can they wilt instead and wonder why, with little fractures of doubt emerging over time?

When they ask, "Why do you love me?" what they are in fact asking is, "What do you see in me?"

Disrespect is entirely different. This is dangerous in a myriad of ways. It means that not only do you see your partner, but you find them lacking and less than; low in worth, little in value. You focus on their faults and imperfections, perhaps look down on them, maybe ignore them and pay them no mind. A relationship in which the partners disrespect each other is in a losing battle with time.

During lockdown, during this intense time of uncertainty and loss (of people, of contact, of routine, of the world as we know it), we need to be <u>more</u> respectful, not less. Sharing space for long periods of time is not without its difficulties. This is especially true when partners have different needs of space and time, of different ways of doing things and managing the new normal.

We should also be kinder to ourselves. To have more respect for who we are and wish to be.

What does self-respect look like?

- Taking care for our physical, emotional and mental wellbeing
- Honoring our dignity
- Seeing perceived failures as growth opportunities
- Understanding that we are an imperfect human who makes mistakes
- Moving away from anything that puts us down

What does it look like when you respect your partner and are respected in a relationship?

- Listening with an open heart and mind
- Making an effort to allow our partner to navigate reality on their own terms
- Not speaking badly to friends about our relationship or our partner
- Honoring confidences and private lives
- Ensuring the sacredness of bonds by being honest and faithful

Respect, to see again.

As if for the first time.

———

Activity

As often as possible, give a sincere compliment to yourself and your partner.

Create a visual memory wall of treasured moments and beloved experiences so that your life together and the respect it deserves is in full sight.

————

Questions for Reflection

Do I respect myself? Why or why not?

Do I respect my partner? Why or why not?

Does my partner respect me?

How can I demonstrate and build the level of respect in my relationship?

35

Journaling the Gratitude In or the Frustration Away

There is significant power in communicating words to ourselves about what's happening on the inside. George Orwell wrote a fantastic essay called "Politics and the English Language". It might sound like it has nothing to do with journaling and the global pandemic, but what he covers in the essay is a fundamental question:

What comes first: thought or language?

He questions the value of a thought that cannot put it into words. And conversely, are our thoughts limited by our own vocabulary? Where do outside influences come to play? And what about the limitations of the English language - sometimes we simply don't have a word for a certain 'thing'.

Here's a short list of just a few of these concepts that we might have in our minds but no word to express, but that other languages have nailed down:

- Bilita Mpash (Bantu) - A wonderful dream. The opposite of a nightmare.

- Cafune (Brazilian Portuguese). The act of running your fingers through your lover's hair.
- Fisselig (German) - Being so flustered that you can't finish what you were doing.

(I just love being able to say, "I can't! I'm fisselig right now!")

Journaling is as much physical as it is mental.

The feeling of holding onto a pen, the sensation of our wrist as it holds our hand upright. The sound that emerges as we scratch letters into words into phrases on the paper. Our eyes take in the sight of the words as much as our brain thinks them. Additionally, we cannot write, especially by hand, as fast as we think. So, journaling has the added benefit slowing us down.

If you're anything like me, you have experienced new emotions on this roller coaster of lockdown and a global pandemic. I often didn't have words to explain to my husband why I was feeling glum, or why I had a new burst of enthusiasm, or even why I had reached (at times) a peaceful state of serenity.

When I started writing about it, the act of thinking forced me to put language onto an internal mystery.

There's a kind of satisfaction in being able to take these abstract concepts and turn them into a physical reality through words in my journal.

A journal can be anything you want it to be. It can fulfill a mix of purposes or you can laser focus on one specific use that you find most helpful.

For example, a journal can be used for:

Gratitude:

List out the small and big things you are grateful for, things that might get missed in the madness of every day.

Exploring emotions:

How are you feeling? Do you know what sparked this feeling? Is the feeling desirable? If so, what can you do to feel it again? If undesirable, what might be some ways to avoid it? What triggers have you uncovered recently?

Ranting:

Your partner driving you crazy? Take it out on the journal instead of on your partner. Everything is fair game here. The goal is to find an outlet for your frustration or anger in order to come back to your partner either having moved on or able to address the actual underlying issues.

An account of the 'everyday':

'Everyday' during the global pandemic is nothing like 'everyday' in normal times. Maybe you want to document it for the future, to have something concrete that has come out of this time that you can share with children, family, friends, or others.

Poetry:

I have been amazed at how many people I have seen turned to poetry as a way to express what they are experiencing during this time. Many of these poems are extraordinarily touching and others show the evolution people are going through during this period.

A side note: your materials may or may not be important.

I personally like to have a beautiful book and a pen that moves on the page without making much noise as it scratches away.

Some people journal on bits of napkins collecting them together into a scrapbook or even just a storage box filled with index cards, each with an idea on it.

––––––––

Activity

Everywhere you look, people will talk about the value of doing something every day in order to turn it into a habit. Depending on your goal, you might not want to make journaling a habit (especially if you use it to express your negative feelings, because who wants to have negative feelings as a habit!)

Instead, I suggest starting with some kind of book so that you have a place where your writing is gathered in a single spot.

Of critical importance here is NOT TO JUDGE yourself nor your writing. We are not writing *War and Peace*, nor Wordsworthian poetry, nor a great biography.

Our inner critic can do us a lot of damage here, so instead, write for the sake of writing and see what happens.

Maybe you just make a list of a few words of gratitude, the flowers you noticed blooming, or the neighbor who mowed your lawn. Maybe you doodle an angry little stick figure. Or maybe you try out some haiku.

––––––––

Resources

If you really want to try your hand at writing but aren't yet hearing your muse, I really recommend you check out the book "Writing Without a Parachute". The methodology created by Barbara Turner-Vesselago called *Freefall Writing*, is one that helps new writers find words and experienced writers overcome blocks.

36

Snappy: The well-timed rest

When I haven't slept well or enough, I am a no-good, horrible, miserable person.

My body forgets how to regulate its temperature and I alternate between boiling and freezing. I cannot tell when I am full or hungry. I feel exhausted, sensitive, and anxious, and I want to shroud myself in a dark place where I don't have to deal with anything or anyone.

Albeit temporary, I definitely go to 'The Dark Side'.

As you can imagine, this doesn't exactly bode well for my relationship.

The only thing that will restore me is a well-timed nap. What do I mean by this? I do not mean a 20-minute power nap, although those can be little morsels of joy. What I mean is that I nap for 90 minutes or even for 3 hours, usually in the afternoon, after my last reserves of energy have petered out.

I have found that there is always a little nook where these precious 90 minutes can be found. You might be wondering, why 90 minutes exactly? Why not 1 hour or 45 minutes? It is simply because I have found that is what corresponds to my sleep cycle - from when I go into light sleep, to deep REM sleep and back out again. The worst thing for me is to take a one-hour or even a two-hour nap since that falls smack dab in the middle of my sleep cycle, and I will wake up groggy and even more exhausted than before.

Trust me, it is not a good look.

If I did this in the office, if I curled up under my desk with a little drool forming on the floor beside me, my colleagues would raise an eyebrow, if not raise the alarm to Human Resources. So, if I was at the office, I would drink obscene amounts of coffee and grit and bear the day, staying in stealth mode as much as possible, that is, not venturing far from my desk, with headphones on and a do not disturb sign. But I would be miserable and not very productive.

The beauty of lockdown is that it is infinitely easier to carve out time to take a needed rest and nap during the day. The nap can be planned around work duties, deliverables, and meetings - not just your own but your partner's as well, especially if they will need to take or make a call or will need to be in a webinar.

After my nap, it feels like a brand new day. Not sunshine and rainbows exactly but I feel better, I have more energy, I am more productive and most importantly, *I am MUCH nicer and have much more patience with my husband.*

A nap is not going to magically fix your relationship or address underlying mental or physical issues. However, as it does for me, it may improve your mood, allow you to function better and be more cognitively and emotionally balanced.

Many studies are finding a good night's sleep is important for the body to heal itself, reduce stress, improve memory, and even to increase life expectancy. However, we might not always get the rest that we need at night.

That is where a solid nap comes in.

Studies too have found that naps can also lift moods, improve alertness, and help with stress.

All of this is great news for you, your partner, and your relationship.

———

Activity

Determine your sleep cycle by 'testing' your naps. Set the alarm for 60 minutes, 75 minutes, 90 minutes, and so on. You will soon figure out what cycle is the one that finds you waking up refreshed and rested.

———

Questions for Reflection

When is the best time for me to plan a nap if I need one? What do I need to have a good, uninterrupted rest - is it earplugs, blinds down or curtains drawn, a white noise generator?

Will my partner need to be on a call or a webinar, or will there be other noises that may interfere with my rest? How can I mitigate them? What is the best way for me to alert my partner that resting is important not just for me, but for us and ask them to support me by reducing noise?

Why am I not resting well at night? Are there underlying issues I need to address such as stress, anxiety, trauma, and depression? If so, where can I seek support for this?

37

Give What You Want to Get, Ask for What you Want

The word "need" is bothersome and can be most unhelpful.

A professor of mine, Robert L. "Bob" Powers (1929-2003), used to say, "When I say I NEEEEEEED something, it really means: I DEMAND it!"

That really struck me, as we always talk about our needs, instead of wants or desires, as if they are as important as survival:

I neeeeed a new coat
I neeeeed a new car
I neeeeed you to do what I say

Of course, we do have needs: food, water, shelter, safety, intimacy. We have needs for affection as human beings in order for us to thrive. But when we tell our partner "I *need* you to..." it may not be received in the way we hope. In fact, by putting it that way, they may feel it as an innate demand and resist, instead of responding.

These days we find ourselves in a particularly stressful situation: lockdown during the COVID-19 pandemic. Our anxiety levels are higher. Our thresholds for stress are lower. What we may have perceived as "needs" in the past may be taking on even greater urgency.

So how can we communicate what it is we *want* - those things that will be soothing or bring us comfort or assistance - such that our partner responds in a caring and loving way to us? And in a way that hopefully will bring us closer instead of frustrated and angry with each other?

First, it is important that we ourselves identify what it is we truly desire. We have to know this before we can ask for it, and not inadvertently demand it, from our partner.

How can they help if we don't know how to communicate our desire to them without making it sound like a demand?

Here is one personal example: I had had a very bad day, at work, and when I got home, got in a fight with my mother on the phone. The result was I was edgy, a bit angry, and ultimately tearful. When my husband came home he asked, "What's wrong?" I went into the litany of problems and frustrations and pain, and he immediately started with: "Well, you should do... and you should try..." etc. You get the picture.

I got more upset because he just wasn't getting what it was I thought I NEEDED, but I didn't even know myself what I needed until he said, "Why are you getting upset with me? I'm just trying to HELP you!"

I said, through tears, once I realized what I really wanted in that moment: "I don't need your HELP, I just want a HUG!"

Thank goodness he was responsive, because I'll never forget that big all-encompassing, warm, supportive hug. I can feel it now, after all these years. Then I realized how to handle these emotional 'needs' of mine: ask for what I want, not as a demand, but with vulnerability, openness, and sincerity.

Related to this is something my husband and I thought of long ago: "Give what you want to get", which is, basically, if you feel as though you want a kiss, give a kiss, if you want to hold hands, take your partner's hand, if you want closeness, sit next to them on the couch. If we want a date night, plan the date night. That's the idea.

It's a small thing, but it can help.

Of course, not always. Sometimes our partner may not be in the mood for a hug, so it is important to be observant and offer what works for them, or even ask them what they want. Every little action can help when we are in the midst of a living, breathing relationship, and especially when we are "locked" up together in the midst of a global crisis.

———

Questions for Reflection

What is it that I truly desire from my partner?

How could I give what I want to get?

How can I communicate what I *desire* without making it sound like a *need*?

38

What Can You Let Go?

Okay, time for a confession here.

This chapter is one I've had to write for my own good.

I've learned the hard way about not being able to do everything many times over in my life. But lockdown brought this to a whole new level.

I'm one of those people who doesn't know how to sit still. There have been recent periods of my life where my day job has had me travel 60% of the time, I was in a semi-professional choir, I went to the gym at least three times a week, I was writing a series of science fiction books, and all the while trying to have a healthy social life, as I'm pretty close to 100% extroverted.

In fact, it was sometime in February 2020 that I was beginning to realize the unsustainability of the volume of my activities. There was a voice in my head (growing progressively louder) telling me I needed to slow down. Stress in my day job was mounting, I had complications with my asthma, and my patience with life in general was starting to wear a little thin.

I distinctly remember a conversation with my husband in the kitchen when I said, "I need things to slow down. But I don't want to give anything up."

I liked all of my activities. I got different kinds of joy out of each of them. Quitting the day job certainly wasn't an option.

But it was becoming apparent to me: by not making a choice, by not slimming down my lifestyle, I was paying for it with my physical and mental health.

Enter: global pandemic.

By mid-March 2020, France was in full lockdown. We needed a permission form to leave the house.

My husband and I looked at each other – it seemed I was getting the slower life, by no choice of my own!

I, therefore, went into lockdown with a really positive attitude. Here was my chance, hopefully temporary and short, where life would be simplified. My activities would be reduced. And I could then reassess later what I wanted to start up again.

Yes, that was what I thought.

No, that is not at all what happened.

You would think a countrywide lockdown would slow many of those extra-curriculars, given all the cancelations and reduction of movement. And yet, what actually happened - and in a way it still blows my mind - was everything ramped up.

My day job exploded as colleagues struggled to move into a working-from-home arrangement. The volume and pressure of the work steadily increased, in many ways due to the pandemic. It never decreased, not for a second.

My choir became a Zoom choir, and suddenly I was in charge of teaching English pronunciation three times a week online to very appreciative amateur French gospel singers.

I took up daily yoga and some running to compensate for the gym being closed.

I increased my daily writing practice, as it allowed my brain to escape from present circumstances into an imaginary world of Queens and fortresses and genetic cloning (it may seem that those things don't go well together, but in my imaginary world, they are perfect friends).

It wasn't long into this lockdown, after a couple of outbursts at my husband that he did not deserve, that the realization hit me square between the eyes.

I was doing too much.

I couldn't continue like this.

I was going to lose it, and things would start falling apart.

I had to stop RIGHT NOW.

I sat down on my sofa, which I was getting really sick of, and I stared at the television, which wasn't even turned on. What could I possibly stop? It felt like people were relying on me. And if not other people, then my body. And if not my body then my intellectual pursuits.

I took a week-long vacation at that time. Actually, it was a week-long staycation. Actually, it was sleeping in and fighting daily misery and fear as the pandemic was hitting a peak in France.

It quite possibly goes down as my least favorite week of vacation ever.

But what it allowed me to do was re-evaluate all of my activities. I have been buzzing like a productive little bee for too long. I needed to let things go. Even when I made a physical effort to stop and smell the roses, I couldn't enjoy them because I constantly felt like there was something else I should be doing with my time. I tried scheduling in the smelling of roses, but you can imagine how that ultimately didn't serve the purpose.

I had to admit something to myself that I am not good at admitting:

I couldn't do it all.

Gosh, even just typing those words here now makes me recoil. I'm still working at understanding what it is in my psyche that drives me to believe that I should be able to do everything. Certainly, when I see my friends in a similar situation, I don't hesitate to give them the same advice that I am trying to give myself by writing this chapter here.

We are finite. Our energy is finite, our time, our abilities, all finite. We have to make choices about what we do with our time. We cannot do it all. I cannot do it all.

Trying to continue doing it all was leaving me less and less time and patience for my relationship.

(Shout out to all of you who are parents or other types of caregivers, as you experience this exponentially greater than me.) So, what could I let go?

I answered the question, I reduced certain activities, and I wasn't happy about it.

But I'm doing better now.

And most importantly, I was the one who decided; it wasn't the circumstances that decided it for me.

There, I said it.

Even as I write this chapter now, I recognize that I have allowed new activities and interests to wiggle their way back into my schedule. Clearly, I am on a journey. There is so much of me that wants to do everything humanly possible in this life, and then I remember – I am finite.

I want to smell the roses and enjoy their scent. I want to walk down the street without feeling like I have to rush (especially since there's nothing to rush for). It's important to me to give my husband the time and energy that he deserves and that enriches our relationship every single day.

It's hard. I want it all. But voilà. Doing it all does not equal happiness (shocking!).

Honey, remind me of this chapter when I forget next time.

––––––––––

Questions for Reflection

These are the questions I ask myself. Perhaps they are useful for you, too.

Have I left sufficient open, unscheduled time and mental space for our relationship to blossom and grow?

Am I experiencing feelings of anxiety, tiredness, and crankiness due to being overstretched and overcommitted?

If so, what can I let go?

39

Confining with Pink Elephants

In another lifetime, I lived in a cooperative housing (co-op) with nine other people in a huge three-floor Victorian house. I still think fondly of the house Wednesday night dinners with loud conversations and guitar singalongs, sometimes to be followed by a trip to our friendly neighborhood sketchy karaoke bar.

At the Cambridge co-op club (of the book fame, *Girl Interrupted*), we held house meetings every other Monday evening, where we discussed anything from the construction of the solar roof to changes on the chore board. But before this, we did two things:

First, we discussed how things were for everyone, using terms of weather. For instance, I might say, "I am under a rainstorm but I glimpse some sunshine up ahead." It was a great way to express what was going on with us without really having to go into detail if we did not want to.

After the weather, we moved on to *pink elephants*. Pink elephants referred to things that were lingering in the air, in the house with us, but it was not yet acknowledged. Was there someone with bad aim in the second-floor bathroom? Was the person in charge of grocery shopping intentionally not purchasing items for people she did not like? And so on. Like magic, the pink elephant, exposed and spoken aloud could now be dealt with and it would disappear.

Confining with pink elephants can leave little room for anything else.

So if it's there, it has to be made real and discussed at the right time (and this doesn't necessarily mean during lockdown).

What are some pink elephants?

- Has the relationship stopped being intimate, but it has gone unsaid?
- Is there little agreement on the future?
- Are there tensions that are hidden and tucked away?

The pink elephants for you are between you and your partner and can be very different than the examples above. But I know this much to be true: the unaddressed pink elephant only gets bigger and more fluorescent, until it just cannot be ignored. Sometimes it explodes. Yet, you'd be surprised how many people just maneuver around it for years and years, trying not to make eye contact with the very core of their issues, concerns, and fears.

So should all pink elephants be fair game during lockdown? No.

I think there are things where a therapist needs to be involved in order for couples to unravel the webs of unspoken things.

But there are perhaps baby pink elephants that can be dealt with. You need to decide this, as it varies from couple to couple.

You might want to let it be until you can get the needed space to process. Or you can use some of the lockdown to muddle through some of it, a little pink piece at a time.

———

Activity

Draw a large elephant on a white paper. Your partner does the same. Write on sticky notes things that trouble you but that are not discussed. Frame it in terms of what you feel rather than what your partner does (this is not the blame game). Place the notes on your respective elephants.

Either put it away or put it in a common space where each of you can read it but you cannot talk about it. It is up to the person who wrote it to raise the issue or not. Select a time when you are both relaxed to discuss, if you choose to do so.

———

Questions for Reflection

Are there unsaid issues in our relationship? What are they?

How do we normally deal with conflict and disagreements? Do we tend to tuck it away?

Are there issues that are better to discuss with a professional?

Am I attacking my *partner* or the *issue*? How can I keep it focused on the issue?

40

Microdecisions: Enjoying a sense of control

There are many reasons not to make big decisions during a period of lockdown.

- Our reasoning is off.
- We don't know what normal is going to look like.
- Our perspective is skewed by present circumstances.
- The future is very difficult to read.

At the same time, we struggle for a sense of control, even control over the things that used to be so easy. Remember when these were the questions we used to ask ourselves?

- Will I go to the gym tonight or not?
- Will we go out for Korean food or for Italian?
- Will we go camping this summer or perhaps a trip abroad?

I find myself longing for the time when Korean or Italian was my biggest question of the day.

Even at the time of writing, I am making plans for the next two years while mentally preparing myself that they may all need to be canceled or changed. My brother's wedding in Italy? Visiting my goddaughter in Canada? Attending critical work meetings in London, England? They could all be out the window!

What am I going to do with all of these air miles I've been saving up for the last five years?

A small antidote to this is the microdecision. For most of us, we have the privilege of making these microdecisions most days of our lives. They are the decisions we don't even recognize, but we take for granted. They are decisions that determine our comfort and state of mind.

Practicing mindfulness or consciousness of these microdecisions puts some control back in our corner. Beware, microdecisions are not something that you will want to be conscious of in the long term, and they're not even for everyone, as they can make the "everyday" feel burdensome with decisions.

However, if you are living in conditions where your "normal" way of being has been stripped, your decisions limited, your sense of control abused, then these microdecisions may help you realize just how much you can decide even during a period of massive uncertainty.

- What sleeping arrangements are your favorite? Do you like spooning? Would increasing the air conditioning make him more comfortable? Is your pillow meeting the needs of your neck? Do you need to look at one that is firmer? Latex? Memory foam? Molded around your neck? Design for side sleeping?

- What lesson from elementary school piqued your interest at the time that you could seek out some free documentary on? The First World War? The way flowers germinate? Burlesque dancers in 1930s Paris?

- Is your kitchen organized the way you want it? What small conveniences could you put in place but make you happy every time you make a cup of coffee or whip some eggs?

- What color nail polish? Purple? Pink? Blue? Glossy or matte? (Do nail polishes come in matte?)

Let's take a look now at microdecisions that you and your partner might be able to make:

- What morning routine suits you best? Are there some little love acts that you could build into that first hour of your morning together?

- Are there specific home renovations that you would like to prioritize?

- What about swapping certain chores?

- Is there a specific type of cooking that you would like to try experimenting with, something very challenging, perhaps? Sushi? Paella? Bratwurst?

- In the interest of keeping this clean, let me just say there are lots of 'activities' that can happen in different rooms of your house, with different implements, or different flavors that you might want to try...

The main idea of these microdecisions is to take back some control in an otherwise uncontrollable situation, to be more conscious of the opportunities in our everyday lives.

———

Questions for Reflection

Where do I have more control than I think? And how does knowing this give me some relief?

PART V

HOW FUN CAN WE MAKE THIS? ROCKING THE LOCKDOWN AND LIFE THEREAFTER

41

Humor Me: The healing power of laugher

There is nothing sexier than a sense of humor. That is probably the reason why instead of the handsome professors in college, I tended to get a crush on the hilarious ones. If they were both cute and funny, you would find me star-struck in the first row.

It's interesting to note that humans are not the only animals who laugh: gorillas, chimps, bonobos all laugh. Dogs certainly look like they smile. It makes me think that there is an evolutionary advantage to laughing. They say there are improved health benefits, so this may be true. Those who didn't have this characteristic simply vanished off; but not all of them, I'm sure you would agree.

Life is absurd. It is especially absurd and topsy turvy at this moment in time. We may have had an illusion of control before but now we are stark naked without even our mythologies to keep us protected.

Laughing, at the very least, takes the edge off. I am not sure I've ever shared the number of jokes, memes, and funny videos more than I did during the lockdown. Jokes about leaving a fortune of toilet paper and hand sanitizers in the will, world leaders who have been photoshopped to look 80 years old, telling us, "You can go back outside now."

Whether by text or phone or video chat, my day brightened up when I connected with friends and we would riff off of each other, laughing and joking around. All I know is that after a good belly laugh, all seems right with the world.

Yet, the paradox is that when we most need to laugh – when we feel stressed, distressed, down, anxious – is when it seems so hard to conjure up anything that would make us want to see the lighter side of things. We don't feel like laughing. It seems impossible. Perhaps even inappropriate.

Which is why we should do it anyway.

But how?

For me, there are certain movies I know always make me crack a smile (Stranger than Fiction) and there are also certain sitcoms (Fleabag) and certain little YouTube videos (Jim Gaffigan's Hot Pockets comedy sketch and reruns of Black Books). They are my giggle jumpstarts.

I think we should laugh loudly in the face of dark times.

As loud as we possibly can.

———

Activities

With your partner, try laughing sessions. It may be forced at first but real laughter is sure to follow. If it seems strange, try doing it along with an online video on laugher classes. They are amusing to think about, but it can get you started on what sounds absurd but will eventually feel great.

Connect with friends who help you to see the silly and fun side of things.

Watch all the little shows and movies that help you smile, giggle, and laugh.

———

Questions for Reflection

What makes me smile and laugh?

What makes my partner smile and laugh?

What shows, movies, or books usually get us giggling?

What can we do that is silly and light and will help us to see the funnier side of things?

42

A Lockdown Love Story: The joint goal of vanlife

Lockdown...it sounds rather scary and unrealistic. Like a movie rather than real life.

How'd we get through it without wanting to kill each other?

Well...a bit about us. Jeff and I have been together two years now. We met on Instagram while I was traveling in the UK. At first, I wasn't interested. I was finally getting to travel and I was, as they say, "finding myself"...at 38 years old. Haha!

He was persistent, though, and I decided to take a look at his pics... he was cute. I gave him my number as I was visiting friends in the UK, only a couple weeks before I was technically supposed to head back to Canada and restart a new life for myself.

We talked...and talked... for about five days.

His laugh made me laugh and I fell for him before I'd even met him. We finally met on a dark Sunday night. He picked me up at my friends and I had never met him in person yet. 10:40 pm and he texts me, "I'm here".

I went downstairs... my friends thought I was crazy... and maybe I was... but it is a happy ending. Ever since then, we haven't parted except for a couple weeks when I went to visit friends in France and he went to Le Mans for a couple days... so a maximum of one month in total of days not being together.

We have traveled to Canada, Scotland, France, and all over England together while he was working. And in the last year we decided we were going to live the "vanlife".

Vanlife: living in a van/motorhome/truck (usually a self-built home) and traveling, a nomadic life.

Jeff's work takes him all over the UK so it seemed pointless to pay rent at a home and have to get hotels as well. And I hate being left behind. I also don't like being in one spot too long.

So we started studying up on vanlife, on tiny houses.... homes made of storage units, huge trucks, little vans...all sorts.

Finally, we decided on a Luton Van, the kind where you can build a bedroom over the cab.

And I believe that is what saved us those months in lockdown.

We don't argue really anyway, and we both have talents and hobbies that are completely separate from each other.

But we were going to be together for three months straight...

Lockdown proved to be harder for some than others. We read all over Facebook about couples that were breaking up over lockdown, realizing they had drifted apart over the years.

I found this very sad, as lockdown for us seemed to go really smoothly. All thanks to vanlife.

Or the plan for it anyway.

He studied day in and day out about everything from the water systems to fuse boxes. We spent days and weeks drawing out designs for this van or that truck.

We couldn't finally come up with a set floor plan though until we decided which van we were going to get. Jeff went to visit a friend a few days earlier, before lockdown happened, and he saw a red Luton van. When he first showed me, I wasn't taken with it because of the size: we had been talking about getting a 25-foot box truck...so the Luton was much smaller than planned. We quickly blew off the idea of the small red one.

A couple of weeks went by. Lockdown was on and he kept going back to this red van from his friends. There were some benefits to this Luton, even if it wasn't what we thought we wanted:

1. Jeff wouldn't have to upgrade his driver's license because it was only a 3.5-ton van and not the 7.5 ton one we were talking about.
2. We could get it now and at least start the process of the van build during lockdown...

So that decided it.

Just the thought of being able to spend this mandatory time at home being able to start and actually plan and build our new future home was the clincher for getting our Luton... who we call Poppy.

The friend left the keys in the van on a side road for a couple of days and we went to grab her so there were no issues of running into people whilst getting her (since the lockdown was still on).

She ended up being a bigger van than I originally thought, quite perfect actually!

So future vanlife is what got us through. Planning something that would be our future home... working on the issues and the needs we needed to be able to live in her... for example, I need a place for my instruments and art supplies... dresses, haha... And he needs to be able to have storage for work tools and that sort of thing.

Lockdown helped us, I think. We lucked out. Having a joint goal and a planned future of freedom and travel is what got us through.

Learn more about Pixie and Jeff's vanlife on their YouTube channel, AlwaysVanAdventure.

43

The Spontaneous Sunflower and Other Little Joys

When we were dating, my husband would send me bouquets of sunflowers that warmed me during the cold autumn months of Boston. I don't remember how the sunflower became our flower but we both gravitated to them and they mean a great deal to us now.

Once in a while, he will still surprise me with spontaneous sunflowers. The last time, he had searched for them on his own and then took me to them, by bike, the very next day at dusk. There were fields and fields of them outstretched like a promise and their golden heads faced west watching the dwindling rays of the sunset. It was a magical moment.

Do you ever just look at your partner and just wonder, what can I do today to make them happy? What can I do that will bring a smile to their face? What would they really enjoy?

It is a wonderful feeling. This is how each of us has answered this question:

- He plants me seeds of plants that I say I like
- He gives me massages on my hard as a rock shoulders
- He always makes sure we have stocks of my favorite chocolates and tea
- I have cold water waiting from him when he comes in from a hot day
- I respect his alone time without any complaints or judgment
- I pick up croissants from his favorite bakery when walking our dog

It is little things and random things and it bonds us closer every time.

During lockdown, what can you do to show your partner that you love them? Here are some ideas:

- Actively listen to them. Put down the phone and turn off the TV. Look at them and really listen.
- Leave post it sticky notes of encouragement and love all around the house.
- Help out with chores that you know they do not enjoy.
- Give them their space.
- Order a movie or book that they've said they've wanted to read or see.
- Offer a massage when you know their back or neck is hurting.
- Tell her or him how much you appreciate them.
- Write a letter all about what they mean to you and the qualities that you admire.
- Watch their favorite show with them for a change.

Check out the chapter on the languages of love. Your partner's way of feeling loved could be different from yours. Find out what is most meaningful to them and try your best to communicate your love in the way they best understand it.

Sometimes, my random sunflowers to him is what I *don't* do, for instance:

- Not making a huge mess when cooking
- Not interrupting him when he is focused with work
- Not starting the espresso machine at 5 am when I wake up
- Not leaving things here and there after I used them

I know this makes him happy and so I try very hard *not to do* these things. I don't always succeed, but I try.

There is a lot to say about effort. Your partner can tell, see and feel when you show them how you feel about them and do things that you know they appreciate.

What is your partner's random sunflower? What would make them smile? And what is yours?

————

Activity

Try one of those 'how well do you know your partner' online quizzes together and discover things that your partner likes and doesn't. Also, try the questionnaire to identify the language of love best spoken and heard by your partner (see the chapter on the languages of love).

Make a list of things your partner said they'd like to do, reach, watch, or try. Ask them what they like and would appreciate.

———

Questions for Reflection

What language of love do I speak? What language of love does my partner speak?

What makes I partner very happy?

What really annoys my partner that I can stop doing?

What random thing can I do that will light up their day?

44

En-COURAGE-ment

Why is our focus so often on what is wrong or what we are missing? Why do we mention mainly the problems instead of having gratitude for what is working?

There is likely an evolutionary reason for this: we had to be on alert for the dangers in life in order to survive as individuals and as a species, and yet we also developed the need to be socially connected and interdependent. We would not have survived as a species had we not been in groups for protection and for food sourcing. We really needed one another, and that is built into our DNA.

First, let us look at what we mean by 'encouragement' and 'discouragement'.

At the root of each of these words is the obvious: Courage.

When a person feels encouraged, they feel the *courage* to "feel capable, to be resilient, to enjoy life, to be happy, contributing members of society (Nelsen 2019). Encouragement is "[t]o have the courage to be imperfect," (Dreikurs 1970) and "to feel free to make mistakes and to learn from them" (Nelsen 2019). When encouraged, people have a belief in themselves that they are of value and worth. Their value is not dependent only upon their actions, but upon who they are as a human being.

On the opposite end, when a person is discouraged, they feel as though they don't have courage, hope, or confidence to move forward in life, nor to be cooperative, contributing members of society. They feel locked in, inflexible, and easily disheartened. They look for their worth externally from others, rather than having an intrinsic belief in themselves and their value as human beings. They are afraid to make mistakes for fear of judgment and criticism.

The roots of discouragement start early, and often with the best of intentions on the part of the parents.

We might believe that if we point out to a child what they are doing wrong then they will know not to do that, and instead will do the 'right' thing. But how are they supposed to know what that is? The way is by encouraging those behaviors that are positive, contributing, caring, and cooperative.

Another method we may use as parents is that of praise, thinking that this will encourage our children. There are pitfalls here, however, as praise focuses more on the external validation of others, rather on the children learning intrinsic belief in themselves. "Praise is not encouraging because it teaches children to become 'approval junkies.' They learn to depend on others to evaluate their worth" (Nelson 2019).

Fast forward now into adulthood and relationships. If we ourselves feel discouraged, then it is much more difficult to be an encouraging partner. If our focus is on the negative in ourselves and each other, and on what doesn't work, then how can either of us feel very good about our relationship? We can both end up feeling discouraged instead of encouraged in ourselves, in each other, and in the relationship.

Two ways to move from that 'felt negative' to a 'felt positive' is by having an attitude of encouraging and using words of encouragement.

By an 'attitude of encouragement', I mean that we *ourselves* need to find those positives in our partners, in our relationships, and in our SELVES. We have to give ourselves a break, and instead of beating ourselves up, focusing on our strengths and valuing those strengths within ourselves. Sometimes it is easier to see it in others before we can do it for ourselves. However you can get to it, the more satisfied and happier you feel, the more fulfilling and satisfying your relationship will be, too.

In his book, *Turning People On: How to be an Encouraging Person,* Lewis E. Losoncy writes that encouragement is an art, and there is a systematic approach we can use to help us become more encouraging and to "create the ideal encouraging relationship" (Losoncy 2000).

According to Losoncy, these include:

Unconditional Positive Regard (see the chapter with that title):

- Accepting and loving our partner for who they are, as they are

A Non-Blaming Attitude:

- Criticizing, and blaming will only further discourage our partner

Empathy (see the chapter on Compassion):

- Really trying to understand your partner through their eyes and heart

Confidence in the Person:

- You have confidence in your partner, even if they may not have it in themselves

Enthusiasm:

- Your expression of enthusiasm in your partner and their willingness to be open with you must be sincere

Non-evaluative listening (see the chapters on Active Listening):

- Don't judge or evaluate what your partner is telling you, but listen and try to understand

The point of encouragement is for us *ourselves* to focus on those positive and wonderful traits and behaviors of our partners, rather than being discouraged by only focusing on the negative, troubling ones.

It can be challenging for us sometimes to find those positives, especially if we are feeling down ourselves, or scared, or stressed, particularly in times of lockdown in the pandemic.

The beauty of the art of encouragement though, is that the more we encourage our loved one, the better we actually feel. It is part of that deep social connection and bond we share.

When we give encouragement, we feel encouraged. When we give love, we feel love. It is one of the wonderful beautiful and magical ironies of being in a loving intimate relationship.

————

Activity

Sometimes the easiest way to start to be encouraging towards your partner is simply to know a few words or phrases of encouragement and start using those.

When you decide to use them with your partner, it will guide you into finding those traits and behaviors you really value and love about your partner, and to communicate them.

Some 'Words of Encouragement' you can try:

Thank you for doing ...... It really meant a lot to me, because.......

I really appreciate how you handled that situation, because.......

When you .... I felt so good, or happy, or loved,......because of your....kindness, caring, attention.....

I just love it when you.... give me a hug, rub my back, get me cherries... etc.....because I feel so ....happy, loved, cared for etc.

In their book, *Love Builders: Powerful Validation Tools to Enhance Every Relationship,* Sidney B. Simon, and Sally "Cecil" Crosiar have a wonderful chapter entitled "The Language of Validation" (Simon and Crosiar 2003).

Here are three groups of words of "encouraging validation" from their book:

"I like you......

> *because you...*
> *for the ways you...*
> *when I see you...*
> *at the times you...*

I respect you......

> *for how you...*
> *for the ways in which you...*
> *every time I see you...*
> *because you are the kind of person who...*

I love......

> *what happens when you...*
> *the uniqueness of you, for example...*
> *the power you bring to...*
> *your special way of being...*
> *the you I see when you..."*

People who encourage focus especially on the other's process, not just the product or result:

You really tried to get that done, but you ran out of time. But that's ok. You'll finish next time.

It is so nice to see how much you enjoy singing...playing the guitar...gardening.

At the end of a long day, or a difficult day, or at just about any time, we can take each other's hands, look each other in the eyes and take turns saying:

One thing I just love (or appreciate... or value... or adore... etc.) about you is...

45

"I see what you mean": Coding messages

He gives me a look across a room and I know what it means. Save me from this 1) annoying 2) pretentious walking achievement-lister and/or 3) boring person who won't leave me alone. At that moment, I saunter over and wrap my arm in his, walking him over to the other side of the room because at that very moment I need to show him something that is 1) fascinating 2) he just won't believe or 3) that he needs to see right away.

We learned early in our relationship to use codes and gestures, that is, little shortcuts in communication that convey in an instant what would require many, many words.

I imagine this is because we come from very different cultures, with very different backgrounds and with different ideas of how to go about things. I am a multitasking extrovert and he is the strong and silent type who likes to do one thing at a time, and to do it well. We rarely, if ever, see things in the same way or initially agree on the approach to life's little conundrums.

Before we had little coded messages, if he was in the middle of a phone conversation and there was a message I needed to relay to the same person on the phone, I would simply say it, with increasing volume, accompanied by a sort of 'look at me' dance. Inevitably, this would be met with 1) a glare 2) shaking of the head, or 3) a turn of the back.

Basically, nothing good.

He would get off the phone and let me know he was trying to listen and ask why I seem to enjoy interrupting him when he's on the phone.

Why indeed?

Simply, it was because I needed to share something with the person as well. But clearly, I was not showing it well. And I was also sharing another message to my partner, one between indifference to his needs and outright disrespect.

So we devised a plan. Now if he is on the phone, I hold up my right hand, pinch my fingers and shake it to let him know that I also need to share information with the person on the phone, whoever they may be. He then asks the person to hold on, listens to what I need to say, and relays it. Works like a dream. Nobody's annoyed and everyone is heard.

During lockdown, especially in closed spaces over many months, codes and gestures can help you see concretely what your partner means, needs and/or is asking.

It can be as creative or simple as you like, it can be about needing space, silence, lunch, it can be to ask for a hug (for us it is outstretched arms to say please let's have the biggest hug in the history of the universe) or just a way to say without saying that I can't talk right now, really focused, will talk to you when I'm free, I love you, and/or please walk the dog.

Codes are especially useful when you just don't have the energy to explain, are busy or in a rush. They avoid hard feelings and generate a kind of bond, liken when you have inside jokes. Instead, you have insider gestures and code bonds.

It shouldn't be too obvious, commonplace (middle finger when annoyed) or mean. It shouldn't really be used to show displeasure (you do not want these gestures to be laced with resentment). You're building a secret language that can save face, time, and get the message across clearly and kindly.

This little tool will surely help you 1) feel connected 2) reduce annoyance and 3) communicate better with your partner.

———

Activity

Together, make up codes and gestures that can help you communicate more easily. Get creative and have fun, make it personal and something just between the two of you.

———

Questions for Reflection

What really works with the way we currently communicate? What can we improve upon?

Do we already communicate with some gestures that are working for us? How can we develop these more?

Are there some issues that keep coming up that we can develop a little code that would help us to understand each other?

Are there some things that go beyond codes and gestures and must really be discussed in detail?

46

A Lockdown Love Story: Working
it out

My girlfriend and I had discussed moving in together and so when the pandemic hit, there wasn't really a big question; it was more like a little question mark. Since we didn't know how it was going to work out, she kept her apartment and moved into mine.

I like to go to the gym and work out regularly. By regularly, I mean every day. I put in a lot of time on strength training. Without working out, it feels like something is missing. I was going stir crazy when my girlfriend's friend's gym closed down, and he was nice enough to give her some machines. It made the apartment cramped but boy, was it was a lifesaver! I pressed the hell out of that bench.

My girlfriend is also pretty fit. She says she's gained the COVID '19', but she looks great to me. She's smart and fun and bubbly and, like me, enjoys going out and socializing.

Her baking and cooking are epic. A lot of cookies and cakes. A lot of saucy and sautéed dishes. She enjoyed cooking it and I enjoyed eating it. We are a perfect match. I think I ate for two, but hey, no regrets.

Not going to the office was pretty hard for me. I like the small talk, the lunch conversations and the face-to-face meetings. In my work, I need to meet with clients alongside my senior colleagues. It is important to develop and maintain rapport and relationships. But now there was none of that.

We didn't love lockdown, but we didn't hate it either. It's brought us closer together in a much shorter time frame. In fact, she's let go of her apartment and we'll both move into our new place across the country, where I just got transferred. A lot of new adventures ahead for us.

No matter where we go, I'm pretty sure you will find us working out in the mornings before chowing down on protein-rich delicious breakfasts that I will cook for the both of us.

47

Boss of the Sauce: Food matters

I am not ashamed to admit that there were times that I have been seduced by tomatoes. Grown in the garden, sun-kissed, "if it was any fresher, you'd have to slap it" tomatoes. A little drizzle of olive oil and a sprinkle of salt. Scrumptious.

It's amazing how good food can help you be in the moment.

I have often thought they should have mindful classes over home-cooked meals – you cannot help but be fully present as you savor sauces, let the avocado melt on your tongue, feel the joy at the simple pleasure of a spaghettini, salt and butter dish, bite into the crumble and feel your tongue dance as it distinguishes between textures.

Cooking and eating during lockdown can really be an opportunity for shared time, to take a pause, to indulge in conversations, and of course, to enjoy delicious food.

Every week, my husband walks down to our local *boucherie*, gets two modest cuts of *tournedos parisien,* and a *galette* of goat cheese. Paired with spinach, potatoes, or a green salad, it has become a very special time for us. It gives us something to look forward to and if I was even the slightest bit annoyed, everything is forgiven, everything is forgotten. To be honest, I can hardly remember my name with all that deliciousness.

If you enjoy cooking, well then, this is your time to shine – there is no better time than during lockdown without the temptation of eating out to try new recipes, perfect your father's special tomato sauce (they don't call him the boss of the sauce for nothing), or revisit tried and true favorites. Same for your partner, if it is they who have heard and answered the call of Julia Child. You can take turns trying to surprise each other and savor items you only dared to try.

Of course, if you both absolutely hate cooking and it feels like a chore, rather than a joy, it is perfectly respectable to stick to simple meals or even (gasp) call in for delivery. Whatever works for you.

The point is to use the cooking and/or eating time to spend quality time together, rather than eat standing up, in front of computers or with the television. Food can bring us together and there is no better time than now to dive into its delectable pleasures.

————

Activity

With your partner, make a list of all your favorite dishes. This conversation will likely evoke pleasant memories too as meals are often tied to events and those who prepared them. Try cooking some of them if you want.

————

Questions for Reflection

Do I or my partner like to cook? If not, can either of us help with the grocery shopping, or cleaning up the dishes?

Are there interesting recipes I've always wanted to try? What ingredients do I need? Where can I find the recipe – friends, online, family?

Am I or my partner on a special diet that might interfere with us enjoying the same meals? How can we share part but not all of the meal without having to cook two separate times?

Do I or my partner have issues with food that could get in the way of us truly enjoying a meal together?

Is it possible to cook and freeze favorite sauces and dishes for easy reheat and more time at the table enjoying and talking?

Do I or my partner love to cook but are really not great cooks? How can we improve? Can we have a candid talk about this?

Is mealtime my time to recharge? Can I have some but not all meals with my partner? Can we have one special meal during the week?

48

Maintain the Mystery

Sooner or later, the real person emerges.

Perhaps after the sixth date. Perhaps after seven months. Eventually, you face the person and not the illusion. The representative that was at the start of the relationship (on his/her best behavior, charming, making an effort, seems to have no evidence of bodily functions) eases into the real person. The guy who burps. The woman who stinks up the room and blames the dog (zoom into unsuspecting dog, eyes wide, tail wagging wondering why his name was mentioned). The guy who snores so loudly, it sounds like Grand Central Station during rush hour. The couple that lives in jogging pants.

All of this is not necessarily a bad thing. As much as the crazy, fun, exciting, and ecstatic start of a relationship is, it is usually a positive sign when it morphs into something stable, real, and comfortable.

However, whether it is after 10 months or 10 years, it's always a good idea to try and maintain a little bit of the mystery.

What does this even mean anyway? And how can you maintain the mystery when you are confined in a one-bedroom apartment with walls so thin, they might as well be made of rice crackers?

I can already hear one of you wondering out loud – honey, *what* mystery? The mystery train left the station a long time ago.

Well, here are a few tips:

- Make a little effort for yourself and for each other. Perhaps it is maintaining a level of hygiene that you know your partner would appreciate. Keeping the beard nice and trimmed? Check. Not staying all day in the clay face mask? Check.

- Keep the bathroom door closed and don't pop in on your partner. Enough said.

- If you know certain foods are going to give you some digestive problems, try to limit them during confinement. Or if you really can't help it, give warning, open windows, light a match or candles. Make it as painless as possible for your partner, and a little head start to move away. And, of course, totally blame the dog.

- Cute *can* be comfortable – they are not mutually exclusive. Once in a while, peel off the yoga pants and put on something fun, flirty, maybe just something different.

Don't get me wrong. I am not advocating for being fake. Basically, maintaining the mystery is that *both of you are trying*. To be kind and patient, to make an effort, to give a bit of privacy, and to maintain your own.

By all means, accept being human and all the awkwardness that can come with that. And chilling in a cocoon of flannel PJs for days on end is perfectly fine. But also, once in a while, why not change into a fabulous dress just to watch Columbo together and see your partner's eyes light up like it's Christmas morning?

It's nice to change it up and keep it fresh. And it's nice when we give a little attention to ourselves, for ourselves and sometimes for our partner.

———

Activity

Plan a day where you both get dressed up to the nines. Perhaps plan it with a take-out dinner and a DVD or streamed movie. Tell each other things you haven't shared before. Look at each other with new eyes.

Pretend you just met recently and you are having your 'First Date'. Dress up, create a romantic setting. Introduce yourselves and tell your story as if for the first time.

Questions for Reflection

Can I make an effort in the way I groom or dress once in a while? Do I like to do that? If not, what else can I do... or not do?

If the walls are thin, can we run the water or insulate noises that I don't want to be heard and my partner does not want to hear?

What would I like my partner to do that would maintain my intrigue for them? Can I discuss it with them in a way that is safe and not a demand/domineering? Can I ask them what they would like to see from me? Do I feel comfortable doing/dressing/trying this?

What can I do for myself and make myself look and feel good for me?

Compromise for Win/Win... or not at all?

How often have we believed that in order to have a healthy cooperative relationship we must compromise with our partner? You know – "Give a little, take a little."

One person can't win all the time, right? Each one should give in here and there and then the relationship will work much better, so we're told. If it turns out that for you, in your relationship, compromise works beautifully, and you both feel that you have achieved what you want enough of the time, then, congratulations! You have figured that out for yourselves!

...Sometimes, though, if that doesn't work, that road to compromise might lead us down a dangerous path...

There are potential pitfalls in compromise. That may sound counter-intuitive, as we have so often been taught that it is a necessary way of getting along with others. However, what if sometimes one person just tends to be the one who is usually the one who 'gives in'? What if over time that person begins to feel some resentment at being the giving one, and not having much chance to have their way?

Sometimes compromise in relationships can work for a couple (see below). But unfortunately, all too often we feel as though we have 'lost' something when we give in or give up for the sake of peace or pleasing our partner.

On the flip side, for our partner who has 'won' in the compromise, while they may feel happy to have achieved their point, they may be unhappy if their partner is unhappy, especially if some behaviors on behalf of the 'losing' partner become angry, resentful or disrespectful. Instead of peace and harmony, instead of grace and giving, both partners end up feeling in a 'Lose/Lose' position instead of a 'Win/Win'! Definitely not what any of us wants!

Let's just look at the terminology.

Lose. Win.

It sounds like a skirmish, or a battle, or a war! As Larry Nisan, therapist and relationship counselor wrote, "Power and politics have no place in intimate relationships, and yet couples often find themselves in such a position" (Nisan 1990).

Unfortunately, compromise can leave us feeling as though we are in a power struggle if the sense of inequality in compromise persists. Now just magnify these feelings during the pandemic and lockdown, and even more hurt and anger and resentment may result.

So how *can* we have a disagreement and end up feeling closer, and not more distant? How can we end up feeling as though each person has been respected and feeling love, not resentment?

One solution is that some couples simply do not even use the word (or the action of) compromise. They negotiate. What is something each person really wants that might require the other person to be put out? I know that our co-author Eden, for example, will go shopping for the house at Ikea alone because her hates shopping. Then her husband is responsible for setting it all up (and generally not complaining about what she has purchased).

What is preferable is *agreement, cooperation,* or *willingness* to find solutions to differences.

Some ideas to help solve this issue in a positive "Win/Win" way:

1. Start with a positive underlying belief: a basic sense of equality of partnership – not one or the other of you is of more or less value (see the chapter on Equality).

2. Not everything has to be solved right away. Of course, we don't agree on everything, but we may be willing to try it our partner's way for a time and then revisit the issue. The agreement is that we will try it 'your' way for now ("I am willing to try it for a week or two or a month") and then we will discuss it again to see how it went and how we each feel. This can work well for issues that are not hot-button or 'hot potato' issues (see the chapter on 'Hot Potato' Topics).

3. Try to see the issue through your partner's eyes with empathy and compassion. Even if you don't agree, at least you can try to

understand where they are coming from, and have a conversation that can end in mutual agreement and understanding.

4. If the issue gets heated, step away and discuss it when emotions have calmed down. We cannot solve anything if our limbic brain is engaged and we have "Flipped our Lids"! We have to calm down and use the great capacity of our prefrontal cortex to come to a solution (see the chapter on the brain).

5. Think of a difference of opinion not as conflict, but as an opportunity to Win/Win/Win. You Win. I Win. The third "Win" is... the Relationship Wins! The Relationship is the third entity in this partnership and it wins as the two of you have worked through a disagreement where both of you can feel good, where you feel that you have worked through something that has brought you closer. Everybody 'Wins!'

6. Have a view to the future. Will this issue be so important a year from now or even longer? Maybe this isn't something that you even need to take a stand on. What difference does it make which movie we actually see tonight in the long run (Coetzee 2019)?

7. Sometimes we really do have strong fundamental differences so that, try as we may, we cannot seem to find common ground. There is no shame in reaching out for help for the relationship. After all, if you needed a medical professional to set your broken leg, why not seek help from a counseling professional if you and your partner just can't find a way for some common ground on a hot-button or 'hot potato' issue?

50

The Unreasonable Request

It makes absolutely no sense. There is no argument that can justify it. It has no logic whatsoever. It is by all definitions, unreasonable.

But it means something to you, you feel strongly about doing it. This is the time when you make your unreasonable request.

This little tool is a great little item to add to a relationship.

It is a request where *you do not have to provide a reason.*

It can be a silly request. It can be romantic. It can be about anything you desire that you know is really not practical or justifiable.

For instance, I will use one of my two unreasonable requests for 2020 towards taking a trip (when we are able to travel again) to this little place I want to visit in Brittany.

The region is not a favorite of my partner's, who believes we will only be wet and cold. However, it seems so beautiful to me, and so I will use my unreasonable request.

This means he has to say yes. Of course, questions can be asked, but no logical justification on my part needs to be given. It is unreasonable, by definition.

The unreasonable request should not be confused by the unrealistic or the dangerous request. You cannot impose anything on your partner – their body and or their wellbeing. And vice versa. You also cannot ask them to go into debt or be at risk. That wouldn't be fair and that is not the point.

It is just a neat little thing that can add a bit of fun and adventure to your relationship. Not all things can be reasoned and so it's nice to have a way to ask for things that are purely because you feel good about it and wish to try it.

———

Questions for Reflection

Would my partner be up for this? Am I up for this?

Could we truly be happy saying yes to each other's unreasonable requests?

What are my unreasonable requests?

What are my partner's unreasonable requests?

———

Activity

Write down things you've always wanted to try and/or places you want to go. Have your partner do the same.

You can place these in a jar, if you like.

Every year, choose one or two to do.

51

Reframing into Gratitude

During times such as this, gratitude can feel like the last thing on our minds.

The world is in chaos; livelihoods and lives have been lost. Why shouldn't we just face the reality of this, and forget this mushy gratitude business?

The answer is pretty easy, in fact.

Being grateful, the very act of finding things to be grateful for, has a positive physiological effect.

The science behind it shows that gratitude has a direct relationship to happiness, that people who are happy are often also people who are grateful.

As theologians like Rabbi Hyman Judah Schachtel and songwriters like Sheryl Crow among many other have said: The trick is not in having what we want, but in wanting what we have. When we want what we have, we see the value in that which surrounds us.

There are things every single day to be grateful for – even the hard things have something in them worthy of gratitude.

I'm not trying to downplay the weight of what some of us are facing during this time. It *is* hard. Gratitude is not about pretending those realities don't exist. Rather, 'reframing into gratitude' is looking at those aspects of our situation that we are capable of viewing from a different vantage point, and then overlaying thankfulness into them.

For example, I was upset that I seemed to be much more emotionally affected by the global pandemic than my husband was. I thought, "How can he be so detached? How can he remain so calm when the whole world is going down the drain?"

But, when I intentionally reframed that into gratitude, it turned into this:

I'm so grateful that when I am at my wit's end and unable to see what's coming next, and when I feel fear about the future, my husband is a stable constant. He's there for me, ready to listen, and remains collected in the face of one of our planet's most challenging periods in recent history.

Gratitude doesn't have to be for big things. Actually, it's in some ways even more helpful for it to be about the little things.

Why the little things? Why not the big things?

> The big things are hard. The big things are big things because they're big. They're overwhelming or frightening.

The little things are easy wins, and yet they add up quickly. It's a bit like earning profit by counting dollars here and there, saving little by little until suddenly, it's very substantial. Not only that, but the emotion of gratitude is not volume-specific. That is one of the great qualities of gratitude: you don't have to be grateful for a big thing in order for the big advantages of gratitude to hit.

You get an immediate return on your investment by taking those itsy-bitsy teeny-weeny little bits of gratitude and sticking them right in that part of your brain which benefits most.

This is also why gratitude journals are so effective. (See the chapter on journaling for some ideas.)

There are some easier places to begin when it comes to gratitude and I don't want to assume that I know what those things are for you, so here are some of mine:

- I have been able to change careers multiple times in my life, to do things I never expected I would have done. And even though there were times that were challenging financially, I was able to find a way to make it work and always have food on the table and a roof over my head.

- A small thing. I am not a morning person. My husband is. He wakes up like that day is the best day that could ever possibly be. I wake up and it's like I experienced Armageddon over the night and need to heal from the experience. Ultimately, this means that he takes the dog out every single morning when he goes to collect his croissant. How I love those extra few minutes when I can lounge around the house in silence, all the while knowing that the dog has been taken care of.

- Also in my gratitude journal is technology. I live abroad. Without ways of seeing my family and friends back home, this would have been an even more trying time than it already was. Instead, I get to see my 94-year-old grandmother and my 5-year-old goddaughter. My brother got to tell me 'face-to-face' that he was getting married. (They clearly survived the lockdown well). And I even still get to see my colleagues as we together carry the weight of our day jobs that have only become more intense since all of this began. Technology has built our camaraderie and our working relationships, and it allows us to see when each other is experiencing stress so that we can be more sensitive to it.

- Next thing I am grateful for? I have got good hair, man. Like, really good hair. I'm not grey (yet), it does that nice beach-wavy thing without my trying, I can throw it up in a ponytail or wear it long down my back and the fact that hairdressers were closed for months on end did not affect the quality of my "coiffe". Awesome!

———

Activity

Go to the chapter on journaling and consider whether a gratitude journal would work for you. If not, it could be as simple as a list when you wake up in the morning. Or pausing in the day to scribble it on a napkin. Or something more detailed - anything you like.

Here's a list I made up just now, to show how easy it can be, and how one thing snowballs into another until the list becomes unending:

- My hair (as already mentioned)
- The feeling of sunshine
- My dog's smile (because she does smile)
- Fresh, local fruit
- Espresso
- Long, flowy skirts that flap in the breeze
- Blossoms on trees as they open into flowers
- Having a job
- Liking my boss
- My mother being willing to write this book with me
- My friend being willing to collaborate on this book with me
- The chance to write a book that I hope might inspire others
- Modern ways of publishing that mean people can access it more easily
- Mint chocolate chip ice cream

52

A Lockdown Love Story: So happy together

The pandemic arrived like tropical rain; drops of water, little by little and then, all at once.

My husband was well aware of the dangers of the new virus and was keeping me abreast of what the scientific community was understanding about SARS 2, a virus with significant overlap in structure with SARS 1.

At work, anti-bacterial gels arrived, hung by elevators and the main doors. A message from Human Resources told us to wash our hands and to be on standby for more news. This was February. Another message went out that a contractor who had visited the office had tested positive. Colleagues spoke in hushed and sometimes not-so-hushed voices in corridors. What is happening? How long does it last in the air, on the surface, in our bodies? Will schools close? Will we?

Then, the country's president ordered a lockdown, and that very evening, I was on the train home to my loves, my husband and our sweet, stubborn dog.

This was March 13th.

I thought (rather naively in hindsight) this should last a few weeks, tops.

Of course, as we now know the lockdown was extended by a month; then two months; then three.

Then just as suddenly, I was requested to report to work on July 1st.

Folded between these dates is our lockdown love story...

Spoiler alert. We LOVED the lockdown. And the more I talk with family and friends, I realize that we are one of the few. Which begs the question, why? After some discussion, we've come up with the following:

We are normally in a long-distance relationship. We have always been in a long-distance relationship. So for us, it was this rare time to be together and share regular days, doing regular mundane things. We felt grateful for this time and I think that formed the foundation of why we felt pretty good about being together all the time.

We have a dog that we love very much and who allowed us to get outside two times a day for his walks. These became sacred times of conversation, musings, sunshine, and exercise. And we developed a routine. I am an early riser which meant I walked our dog in the morning and would pick up the baguettes on the way. I had short conversations with our lovely *boulanger* which, as a pretty social person, was a good thing for me. Most evenings, we did the walks together.

The way our apartment is arranged allowed us to have separate working areas – he has his desk in one room and me in another. That means we each had our own space and were not climbing all over each other.

Lucky for us, just before the lockdown, we had invested in wireless sound-canceling headphones. It was intended for me since I share an office and there was usually someone on the phone. Since I like quiet mornings and my husband likes to listen to the news, he used the headphones and got his news while I sipped my coffee and wrote in peace.

We would take breaks from our work to have lunch and tea. This connected us in conversation and allowed us to discuss how our respective days were going.

He let me do my thing and I let him do his thing. Whether it was reading, napping, listening to music and podcasts, playing video games, or dancing, we just did what we liked when we needed to relax a bit. The key is that we didn't nag each other about it. It was just understood.

He is an incredible cook. A thousand times better than me. So he would cook these delicious meals and I would be so grateful. I also cooked and enjoyed it but I secretly loved it when he offered to make the meal for that day.

I did things that he didn't love to do like organize the living room, fold the laundry, or do a deep clean on the kitchen. And he did things I didn't like to do like the groceries and dishes. We have kind of found our footing on chores.

We had date nights on Saturday which gave us something to look forward to. Nothing major, just a favorite show and cuddles.

I decided to get strong and focused on fitness. But I didn't force him to join me or scold him about staying active. I just stuck to my goals and felt great seeing little baby muscles where before, I had none. On his own, he started biking and running but it came from him, not any push from me.

Working from a distance suited me in that I could do the work in the times in which I had the most energy and could nap when I needed to. I was very productive and happy as a result of working around a schedule that made sense for me.

He introduced me to films I had never seen before. His favorites like Subway, Grand Blue, Nikita, Leon, 5th Element, all 9 episodes of Star Wars, and classic Marlon Brando films. We savored them together, like fine wine, and had many conversations about plots and subplots.

We are very affectionate and so it was wonderful to be in contact as much as we wanted. We also have a dog who loves belly rubs and pets and so all that was like a little therapy.

I practiced the piano and was developing my talent which felt great. I was proud when I moved a song from choppy to decent to 'wow, that sounds good.'

We didn't take each other for granted. Somehow, I always felt lucky to be with him, to have him with me, to share our lives, to share this strange time together. He's my person and so this feeling of being in some fairytale love story seemed more real than ever.

If we got annoyed at each other, we squashed it right away. No grudges, no yelling, no meanness; we just sorted it out. We talked it out.

We were lucky not to have anyone close to us be impacted by the virus (health-wise) and so that kept it at an arm's length somehow.

With noise pollution on halt, the song of the birds was clear and amplified. Every morning was like a serenade and we would pause and pay attention.

We had virtual face-time with family and friends that included a glass of wine or pastis, dressing up, and games like Trivia Pursuit and 80s Facts. We loved seeing everyone and sharing some fun times and laughter at a distance.

We know the pandemic has hurt many people. It has tragically killed over a million people at the time of writing. The reality is not lost on us and that the world will never be the same. It *should* not be the same. It has changed our relationship to nature and to each other in fundamental ways.

Yet, we also know that during these uncertain crazy strange times, all we did was cling onto each other and our little furball and face it together as a little family of three. And that made all the difference.

53

Let the Birdie Be: Choosing your battles

First, it was the birdie.

Then it was the racket used to get the birdie down.

Then it was the volleyball used to get the racket down.

Then it was two plastic arrows we sent up with the bow to get the racket down.

There they were, all stuck in the big oak tree, looking down at us mere mortals, untouchable. Instead of one problem, we now had five.

That's often what it's like when we decide to take on every little thing, indiscriminately.

Instead of letting the little thing go, we go after it with gusto. It then creates another dilemma and so on and so forth. Because it's never just one little thing is it? These little things have a way of being like a chain of islands – you see the surfaces but they are all connected underneath. The key is to get to the root and work that out instead of picking at the superficial issues.

Day to day, choosing our battles is essential. I would even say it's one of the most important skills to develop in a relationship.

Why?

Because if you decide to take on and argue about every little thing that your partner does and says that annoys and troubles you and vice versa, you could very well spend most of your relationship doing just that.

And to what end?

To constantly aim to 'win' arguments is to succeed at the battle to lose the war, so to speak.

This is not to say there are no disagreements, discussions, and arguments worth having. There are. There most certainly are. And it is up to you to decide what are important points of tensions and disconnect that must be addressed. And in fact, these should not be arguments *per se*, but rather conversations, with an eye to reconciling differences and compromise.

I've also noticed that when we're content and happy within ourselves, we tend to overlook these so-called 'faults'. But if we are not settled in our own body and mind, then life is under a giant magnifying glass of our critical gaze. Sadly, it is usually the one nearest to us who gets the brunt of the criticism, complaint, sarcasm, and even contempt.

Also, the minute voices are raised, it's over. Because nobody can listen, truly and deeply listen to what you are saying if the way you are saying it aggressively. Who wants that? Certainly not anybody I know.

So if it gets to the point of frustration, take a pause. Have a code to say (see the chapter on coding messages), which means 'I can't talk about this right now, I'm too emotionally charged'.

Certainly, do not argue to the point where you are hurt and angry and both of you say things you do not want to say. Hurtful words can be scarring and hard to recover from.

Really, just avoid it altogether.

There is another thing that happens when you decide to be (shall we say) enthusiastic, about taking on each other's every flaw and things that vex you. You get tuned out. It's the same thing over and over again that it almost becomes commonplace. You become the person who cries 'you leave a big mess when you cook and it's annoying.' The first time, okay. The twentieth time will be met with an eye roll with no real motivation to change.

A snowball of passive-aggressive actions can also begin to grow. It's something like this: 'I know [this] bothers you, you pick on me about it constantly and I'll do just that to get on your nerves'.

The racket and volleyball are now both up in the tree.

Interestingly, a few days later, the racket had fallen down. Given a bit of time, this is also what often happens to little grievances. They can disappear and evaporate given enough time or seen in the light of morning.

During lockdown, especially after several months, the way your partner *breathes* can get annoying. I mean do they really have to inhale like that? But try to let it go. Be selective. Instead, write it out, meditate it out, read it out, or exercise it out. Pick and choose your battles that are really important to you and to the health of both your wellbeing and your relationship.

Let the birdie be.

_____

Activities

Place a notepad and a box on a counter. Decide on a period of time (a week or longer) to write out your grievances and put them in the box. Indicate on the note what is important to you and what is something you can live with. At the end of the time period, open them with your partner when both of you are relaxed, and discuss the important issues. Put aside the 'can live with' items. Leave them in the box if your partner is interested in reading them (and vice-versa). To better know what is important and what is minor, use color-coded notes.

Once in a while, ask your partner, "What is something I do that really gets on your nerves?" You might be surprised. It could be something that you had no idea was ruffling their feathers. But talking is the best way to uncover these things. And talking without judgment and in a peaceful moment can go a long way.

_____

Questions for Reflection

Will it matter a week from now? A month from now? A year from now? Five years from now?

How can we create a win-win situation instead of a win-lose situation?

Why do I care so much about this issue? What is at the root of it all?

What things that keep resurfacing really need in-depth conversation?

Is fighting a way of me getting attention? Is there another more positive way to ask for what I need?

Are there patterns from previous relationships or my family background feeding my urge to bicker? How can I address this in a healthier fashion?

54

The Art of Locking It Down

I once read about a study that researched couples, their hobbies, and the impact it had on their relationships. Some preferred stationary hobbies like playing board games. Others were more active – they would hike, ski, or run together. Those who were more active had stronger bonds, apparently due to endorphins produced during exercise and other hormones.

I always found this study fascinating and it made me think about my own relationship.

We love hikes and walking so that was good. But we also love doing puzzles and quiet evenings watching movies.

Well, as long as there is a balance, I thought.

However, no matter what we do together, I do notice that whenever we add music to our still or heartbeat-raising activities, the time spent is simply better. Even if it is just doing the chores with a little Ray Charles number in the background or walking the dog listening to Bob Dylan and Abba.

While we have very different tastes in music, there is a nice little overlap in our preferences. Sometimes we just listen, sometimes we sing along. For me, if I really love it, I try to learn it on the piano. I make a mental note of the songs he says he likes, so I can find the sheet music.

Art is weaved into the tapestry of our love affair; little concerts by folk artists, symphonies, theatre, dance, and literature, we relish being cloistered in the drama of it all.

So what to do now that the lockdown has put a damper on all gatherings, artistic or otherwise?

If so inclined, it is possible to make your own art. I think that is why the piano means so much to me. To be able to create something from nothing.

It has given us both time to dive into literature, into the perfectly formed sentences of the greats and the newcomers. The kind of books that give you a little heartbreak when the last page of the last chapter is read. How you miss those characters.

In this time, we've become very selective about the films we watch and go out of the way to see those films that have really formed us and rest somewhere between nostalgia and dreams.

We do not paint and haven't done so during lockdown but I know of couples that have taken it up and find it sparks joy in them.

A dear friend of mine plays the guitar and sings her Bob Marley renditions. It makes us smile and think that *yes, everything is going to be alright.*

The Arts are healing. For instance, music has been shown to produce endorphins and release stress. The Arts have a way of taking us somewhere else, putting us in the shoes of others, whisking us away to magical places where creation happens. It can be our voices, our instruments, our imagination. Whatever the expression of art that adds a layer to your lives, open yourself up to it. Who knows? It may even get your heartbeat going...

———

Activity

Dance, sing, play, act, and read without abandon. Together or not, just go for it.

———

Questions for Reflection

What art form have I always wanted to try?

Are there online classes I can take to learn?

Are there artistic hobbies my partner and I can enjoy together?

55

Intimacy (The F-Word)

Anyone who has ever been in a relationship will tell you that intimacy is not sex and sex is not intimacy. As Amy Color says in her Ted Talk, intimacy is really about another F word: Feelings.

- Do we feel connected?
- Do we feel emotionally close?
- Do we feel psychologically close?
- Do we feel safe?
- Do we feel trust?
- Do we feel trusted?
- Do we feel okay to be vulnerable?
- Do we feel heard?
- Do we feel we can share our true selves?
- Do we feel understood?
- Do we feel affirmed?
- Do we feel loved?

According to a study by Douglas Kelley (2019) study participants said that intimacy was about:

- the little things *and* the big things that make you feel a sense of attachment and togetherness;
- feeling that the person 'gets you';
- presence without judgment. Ultimately, it is about acceptance;
- valuing each other and feeling and giving worth;
- transformation and expressing one's true self.

This is not to say that intimacy is outside of touch and that physical closeness does not come into play. It does. But to feel and be truly intimate, the focus is on the relating and the relationship. It is the closeness of all the other aspects that nurture and connect us deeply on a physical level. Another way of saying this: emotional intimacy and physical intimacy together is truly the best combination.

Now for some people, and in particular men (but of course, not all men), sexual intimacy is what makes them feel closeness and emotionally intimate, ready to share and be vulnerable.

Are you able to connect with your partner physically to facilitate the emotional connection even if you are not 'in the mood'? It may well worth the try. I remember our pre-marriage counselor sharing a story of a woman who was annoyed that her partner desired sex once a week. She thought it was too much as she was busy with many responsibilities; but her partner thought there was *not enough* sexual intimacy. The counselor suggested chores were shared more equally and that they actually INCREASE how often they were physically intimate. Ultimately, she had more time, was less stressed, and happier. He was also much happier and (get this) more willing to help out. Take that from what you will, but for some people the chicken (physical connection) comes before the egg (emotional connection).

So, what can you do to have and stay emotionally connected in and out of lockdown?

You can talk, *really* talk and have meaningful conversations, opening up, and sharing things you haven't shared before. You can show your partner in a myriad of ways that you value them. You can be present; fully and truly present - not just there in person but mentally miles away, ticking off to-do lists in your mind. You can listen and be vulnerable, you can hold hands or dance on the kitchen floor. You can play. You can share fantasies, fears, hopes, and dreams. You can be yourself, your true self, and welcome who they are, *their real them*, without pretense or judgment. And you can initiate physical intimacy.

It's interesting that it can go either way and, in many ways, it is a *choice*. Spending a lot of time together can create distance or it can help to build that connection, that perhaps has frayed over the months or years. It can build isolation or it can foster closeness. It can weaken desire or it can strengthen a nascent bond.

So why not use this as an opportunity to feel that this person here is YOUR person and you are theirs...the good and the bad...that you are stuck in this together and that there is no one else you would rather share it with.

———

Activity

Try writing letters telling each other what you love about them, why you value them, and the ways they have enriched your life. It takes time and effort to pen down feelings and it is something that can be read over and over.

If this feels a bit too much, start with little notes with things you admire, a moment you shared that was very special, something you can't wait to do with them.

———

Questions for Reflection

When do I feel most intimate with my partner? When do they feel most intimate with me?

Do I have difficulties with intimacy? Why might that be? Is it something I can work on?

Are there aspects of me that I do not wish to share with my partner? Why?

Are there questions that we can ask each other that can help us communicate on a meaningful level and get beyond the surface?

What gets in the way of our intimacy?

What facilities our intimacy?

———

Resources

Amy Color, Ted Talk - Better Intimacy for her, better sex for him and vice versa

The 36 Questions that lead to love: http://36question-sinlove.com/

56

Good, Simple Fun

Well, I don't know about you, but this whole pandemic thing has been a pretty intense freaking experience.

As a friend of mine put it so eloquently, s*** is heavy.

It's so true, s*** really is heavy. Super heavy.

So much of this book talks about how to handle things that are heavy. That's because heavy is hard.

So let's have some good, simple fun.

Below is just a starter list of little things to play on the light side. We were all kids once. We've all played with varying degrees of light-heartedness. Why not give one of these a try to cast some new light on your relationship in otherwise heavy times?

. . .

The Home-Bound Treasure Hunt

Simple. Think of a prize.

A pizza dinner with Coors Light. Maybe a little bit of sexy time. That new app your partner really wants. That's your treasure.

Now write up little notes to take your partner around the house. The notes can be everything from bland and everyday (where do we keep our coldest meat) to much more personalized and specific (beneath the gift you gave me on our first anniversary that I under-appreciated at the time and now have grown so fond of).

I personally think a minimum of five is good. If you're really creative, have some hints that could allude to two different places. You know, to draw out the fun a little longer. And then, when your partner arrives at the prize, ta-da!

Points for consideration:

•Be specific. Nothing is more annoying than a treasure hunt where at least ten different places could fit the hint.

•Don't be too specific. Great frustration can grow from not knowing the answer because it's so obscure that only Einstein between the ages of twelve and fourteen years eleven months could figure it out.

•Get creative with your locations. Body parts count...

•Give hints! If your partner is struggling, don't let it go on for too long, even if it seems obvious to you. Of course it's obvious to you, you wrote it! The point here is to have fun. A little self-deprecating "Oh yes, I guess that hint isn't very clear..." can go a long way.

. . .

Karaoke!

Bless YouTube and its prolific karaoke list! Start with some songs your partner really loves, if they are feeling hesitant about it. A couple of drinks maybe (as long as addiction isn't a problem...) and go for it!

"My heart with go ooooooooooooon..." (My husband has banned that one from the playlist)

The Custom Music Message

Let's take what was karaoke and move it to a whole new level. The custom music message for someone you both love.

Good news, you don't need to be musically talented for this one! Sure, some harmonica, drums, pots and pans and whistles are all fair game.

• Take a song you particularly enjoy, both of you, and rewrite the lyrics dedicated to a family member, friend, or other loved one. Write new lyrics in homage to that person.

• An easy way to get around the challenge of background music is to use a karaoke version of the song on YouTube. That way, any personal instruments you may have simply add an additional effect without being reliant for your serenade-ee to recognize the song.

• Having trouble writing lyrics together? Each of you can take a stanza.

• One of you more gifted in writing lyrics while the other has a particular penchant for playing saucepan snare drum? Divvy up the responsibilities.

Not only do you give a gift to someone you care about, but you enjoy the time together along the way.

Name That Smell!

Super easy, gather up some smelly things in your home. You know, we all have them.

Wait. Don't go too crazy. Ten to fifteen items is ideal. Soaps, scented creams, sauces, smelly socks... (you can decide where you want to draw the line). I think you can see where this is going from here.

One of you is blindfolded. The other presents the scent.

Another take on this one, Name That Taste!

Dirty socks are highly discouraged. I may have opened up a Pandora's box with this one...

57

A Lockdown Love Story: "If all else fails, get a puppy!"

As the senior (in age) member of this writing team, learning that we were in a pandemic, meant major shifts in thinking.

I definitely had some sense of gratitude for a safe life in the first more than two-thirds of my life span: no World Wars to live through, no Great Depression, no famine, as many others have had to endure (including my own parents).

So yes, gratitude was part of what helped me adapt. The thought that if *they* could go through those kinds of losses, perhaps never seeing loved ones again, then we can make it through this. After all, it's just a few rules of distancing, wearing masks, staying isolated, and learning to wash our hands for 20 seconds. (Nothing like singing Twinkle, Twinkle Little Star in my head to get to 20 seconds!)

Yet there was also a lot of fear, sadness and resentment, and some 'poor me' thinking: What will the remainder of my life look like? Will I have horrible losses of loved ones? Will I get sick or die before I'm ready? Why can't I just live the rest of my life without all this fear of death?

At the same time, I had gratitude that my beloved husband, Larry, who passed away in 2008 didn't have to endure this. And yet I so wished for his wisdom, his sense of transcendence and philosophical-yet-pragmatic, thought which I think could have helped me through this.

With great fortune, though, I met a wonderful man named a few years ago who also had lost his beloved spouse, and I was able to find love for a second time in life. We faced this global crisis together, with all the ups and downs it entailed, even though everything felt topsy-turvy, like Alice in Wonderland.

We had planned a beautiful trip for March 2020 to Spain and France to visit my daughter and son-in-law. We had packed our bags. We had booked our airport limousine. Then we got the email: Lufthansa had changed our connecting flights in Spain so we would have a 3-day layover to get from Madrid to Seville, but if that did not suit us, we could cancel our flights with a full refund. My partner saw the writing on the wall: even if we went could get stranded over there.

So, with heavy hearts, we canceled our trip.

At first, we were so upset, resentful, sad, and deflated. But then as the daily news from Europe reached us - COVID in Italy, Spain and France growing exponentially worse - we were so relieved that we didn't go. We felt as though we had dodged a bullet.

But what did that leave us with?

Instead of Europe, we took a few days in Frankenmuth, Michigan - the most European town within driving distance I could think of. We had a lovely time, even though in March it was quite empty of tourists, and news of COVID was remote – only two suspected in the northern peninsula. We came home, having had a sweet few days away; not Europe, but we certainly made the most of it.

Within two days of returning home, the border between Canada and the US was closed!

By then, everything had changed. We had to self-isolate for two weeks because we had traveled outside Canada. My partner's work in the entertainment industry completely tanked. All my clients had to cancel. We were left having to face the great fear of the unknown, invisible enemy.

So what to do?

We had already been discussing for six months the possibility of getting another dog, although life was good and quiet - maybe too quiet – without one. Gypsy, a miniature dachshund and our last little dog of the four we'd once had, died in March 2019. We had both had dogs our whole lives, since childhood, and that was a great many years combined between us!

One morning after we got home from Michigan we talked about it. No Europe, no traveling in the near or perhaps far future, no going out to dinner or a movie. What should we do?

Well, as it says in the title, all else failed. so we decided to get a puppy! We knew what breed we wanted, as we'd had a little Schnoodle (mini Schnauzer-Poodle) before, and while we wanted to rescue one, none were to be found. Thankfully, I had heard of a wonderful breeder, and as luck would have it, she had a litter of puppies born in January and ready to be adopted within a couple of weeks. So on March 20, 2020, our little puppy arrived by cargo – the last flight she could get him on before it all shut down! We decided it really was meant to be!

Now we have had this puppy with all the ups and downs (mostly ups) of puppyhood. He's full of unconditional love for us and us for him. But what really helped is that he doesn't know there is a pandemic out there! He didn't know we were in lockdown. All he wants is to do his 'business', eat, drink (water) and play, play, play!

The joy this little dog has brought us is immeasurable and will continue to be so beyond these terrible days of uncertainty and insecurity. Life does go on. And so does love. Even in lockdown.

Letter to Readers

Dear Reader,

We wrote this book to give some helpful tips to couples who found themselves flung together for long periods of time during the pandemic. Some of us struggled, some of us blossomed, and most of us were in the in-between spaces.

As we write this, the first wave of the health pandemic is over in Europe with a second wave starting, it is still very high in North America and in parts of Asia and South America. A viable vaccine has not yet been created. Who knows what the future holds? We can hope for the best but there may be another lockdown on the horizon.

Time together can also revive lost feelings and spark the romance of the first months and years. But as we all know, spending a lot of time under the same roof does not necessarily mean spending quality time. Fractures in relationships can crack under the weight of various stresses. These processes are as complex as relationships themselves.

You may learn during the lockdown that the person you are with is not the person for you. That you do not seem to agree on the basic things or that you do not find joy in each other and in each other's company. Not superficial things, not little arguments, not minor grievances but the real true blue deep aspects that are the foundation of two people making a life together.

If you find you have grown apart and need to go your own ways then steep your feelings in kindness and sympathy. Try not to make this decision in the heat of the moment, perhaps not even during the lockdown. Take some distance, if you can. But also know that couples sometimes grow apart and it is not always for lack of trying.

On the other hand, if you are with your person and just need some ideas and tips, then we hope this book has helped some. It's hard to see relationships, especially our own, and the perspectives of others can sometimes help to give a little clarity. That is why the lockdown love stories are weaved throughout. Perhaps you see yourself reflected in some of them.

We hope this book has meant something to you and has given you some ideas and maybe even some hope. Pass it around, send it to your friends, and use it up.

With love,

The Love In and Out of Lockdown Authors

Appendix: Suggestions for finding a counselor

Each country has professional organizations that may have therapist, counselor, or psychologist directories.

Some examples include:

• APA –American Psychological Association has a link on their website where you can search for a Psychologist

• CRPO – College of Registered Psychotherapists of Ontario have a search you can do to find a psychotherapist.

• BCAP – British Association for and Psychotherapy also helps you find a therapist.

These are only three examples of many you can search for online.

Your doctor can be an invaluable referral source as well. Some types of counselors or therapists might even be covered by your insurance.

Remember though, that no matter whom you choose, the most important aspect of your work with that professional is the therapeutic relationship. You must feel a level of comfort and trust with your counselor.

If you get started and you don't experience that, you can look for someone else with whom you are more compatible.

As therapists we do understand that, and we do not take it personally if you need to find someone else.

Appendix: References

Adler, Alfred. 2011. *Social Interest: A Challenge to Mankind*. Eastford, CT: Martino Publishing.

Chapman, Gary. 2015. *The Five Love Languages*. Chicago: Moody Publishers.

Coetzee, Zoe. 2019. "Compromise in Relationships: 12 Secrets to bending instead of breaking." Elite Singles Magazine, 23.05.2019. https://www.elitesingles.ca/en/mag/find-match/compromise-in-relationships.

Color, Amy. 2018. Ted Talk, "Better Intimacy for her, better sex for him and vice versa." March 2018. https://www.ted.com/talks/amy_color_better_intimacy_-for_her_better_sex_for_him_vice_versa.

Dreikurs, Rudolf and Margaret Goldman. 1986. *The ABC's of Guiding the Child*. Chicago: Alfred Adler Institute of Chicago.

Dreikurs, Rudolf: reference to "the courage to be imperfect" in a speech delivered by Dreikurs in 1970 at the University of Oregon in Eugene.

Hossenfelder, Sabine. Feb. 6, 2020. YouTube Channel: Science without the gobbledygook Lyrics and song "Ivory Tower." https://youtu.be./T_ckiLhppik.

Kelley, Douglas. April 2019. "Experiencing Intimate Space: Six ways people experience intimacy." https://www.ted.com/talks/douglas_kelley_experiencing_intimate_space_six_ways_people_experience_intimacy

Losoncy, Lewis E. 2000. *Turning People ON: How to be an Encouraging Person.* Sanford Florida: InSync Press.

Merriam-Webster online Dictionary: https://www.merriam-webster.com/dictionary/compassion.

Neff, Kristen. April 2011. Self-Compassion; William Morrow.

Nelsen, Dr. Jane. "Encouragement: What does it mean and how is it done?" Blog 05/06/2019 https://www.positivediscipline.com/articles/encouragement-what-does-it-mean-and-how-is-it-done

Nisan, Larry. 1990. *Love in the Making.* Excerpts from the unpublished papers of Larry Nisan.

Orwell, George. April 1946. *Politics and the English Language.* London: Horizon.

Rogers, Carl R. 1961. *On Becoming a Person: A Therapist's View of Psychotherapy.* Boston: Houghton Mifflin Company.

Rogers, Carl R. 1977. *Carl Rogers On Personal Power: Inner Strength and Its Revolutionary Impact.* New York: Delacorte Press.

Rogers, Carl R. and Richard Evans Farson. 2015. *Active Listening.* Eastford, CT: Martino Publishing.

Rogers, C. R., and Stevens, B., Gendlin, E. T., and Shlien, J. M., and Van Dusen, W. 1967. *Person to person: The problem of being human: A new trend in psychology.* Lafayette, CA: Real People Press.

Siegel, Dr. Daniel J. 2001. *Mindsight, The New Science of Personal Transformation.* New York: Bantam Books.

Siegel, Dr. Daniel J. 2012. "Dr. Dan Siegel presenting a Hand Model of the Brain". YouTube, Feb. 29, 2012. https://youtu.be/gm9CIJ74Oxw.

Simon, Sidney B. and Sally "Cecil" Crosiar. 2003. *Love Builders: Powerful Validation Tools to Enhance Every Relationship.* Lincoln, NE: iUniverse Inc.

Turner-Vesselago, Barbara. 2016. *Writing Without a Parachute: The Art of Freefall.* London: Jessica Kingsley Publishers.

Acknowledgments

Eden

Mon amour, confinement was possible because I was confined with you. I miss my amazing Canadian rock star cheerleading friends, but hearts know no distance. Thank you for your constant encouragement and unending love, no matter what hair-brained scheme I might have. Thank you to those who shared their love stories with me. I know you all go much deeper than these pages could ever convey.

Big thank you to my co-authors, for jumping on board with enthusiasm. Mom, well done. I may regress into a teenager when I'm home with you, but it's been great to be your peer on this project.

Christine

I have the deepest debt of gratitude to my four great Adlerian teachers:

Alfred Adler (1870 -1937), and Rudolf Dreikurs (19897-1972).

Harold Mosak (1921-2018) was my professor, my mentor and my beloved friend who taught me, guided me, and supported me in my career, and in my life. Without him, I could never have been the therapist, and person, that I am today.

Larry Nisan (1949 – 2008), my husband, my best friend, my soul mate, my co-counselor and my co-parent. His passion for helping children around the world inspired so many of us, myself included. He was a great Adlerian teacher to people of all ages. It was his abiding love as a father, son, brother, and husband that drew me in for over 40 years to drink from his invigorating laughter-filled and life-affirming well of wisdom, knowledge and love.

And finally, to my daughter: thank you for inviting me to join you on this book!

Anaïs

Merci à *mio Francesco* dont l'amour est sans mesure. Merci également à Laura and Derek et à Gulyenne et Jacques dont les 43 et 60 ans de mariage sont des sources d'inspiration pour nous tous.

About the Authors

Eden E. Wolfe is the *nom de plume* for Elysia Nisan, who works for a children's charity by day and writes dystopian science fiction by night. She long ago abandoned Canadian winters for the south of France, fulfilling her childhood dream. She still doesn't know what she wants to be when she grows up, but the voyage of growth has been a great one so far. She's married to a juggling, unicycle-riding, balalaika-playing extroverted Frenchman who has come to love her fluffy golden retriever. Learn more about her fiction writing at www.edenwolfe.com

———

Christine Nisan is a Registered Psychotherapist in the province of Ontario, Canada, and has been practicing counseling and psychotherapy for over 30 years. She is deeply grateful to her clients over the years who have entrusted her as an equal partner in their quest to grow, to overcome hurdles, and to move towards their goals and dreams in life. In her personal life, relationships and love have always been her priority. Her roles as a daughter, wife, mother, friend, and citizen of humanity, are central to her essence. These relationships filled with equality, respect, joy, and love are at the core of her life's journey.

———

Anaïs Danesi spent many hours of her childhood at the Gladstone Public Library on Bloor Street in Toronto, where she became enchanted with words, stories and books. She is madly in love with Francesco, with whom she shares Charlie Epsilon, their cute but very naughty dog. Anaïs holds a doctorate degree from Harvard University and believes in dragons and the healing power of kindness.